HORACE BUSHNELL
AND RELIGIOUS EDUCATION

John Andrew & Son, Boston.

Horace Bushnell.

From a daguerreotype taken in 1848.

HORACE BUSHNELL
and
RELIGIOUS EDUCATION

By
A. J. Wm. Myers, Ph. D.
Department of Religious Education
Hartford Seminary Foundation

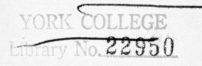
1937
MANTHORNE & BURACK, Inc.
Boston

Printed in U. S. A.

DEDICATED TO

ALL WHO ATTEMPT TO BE
IN ANY SENSE
GOD'S EXPERIMENTERS

"I fell into the habit of talking with God
on every occasion."
—Bushnell.

TABLE OF CONTENTS

HORACE BUSHNELL
AND RELIGIOUS EDUCATION

CHAPTER I

INTRODUCTION: ONE OF GOD'S EXPERIMENTERS

HORACE BUSHNELL was the first outstanding leader in New England to declare publicly for the Magna Charta of Christian Nurture and to compel the attention of the church and the public:

The child is to grow up a Christian, and never know himself as being otherwise.

This doctrine is not new. It is as old as the Christian church.

This conception was full of dynamite threatening the very foundations of New England theology as expounded in catechisms, the New England Primer, and such preaching as that of Jonathan Edwards.

Orthodoxy fought back with every weapon in its arsenal, and with skill and cunning, but it failed. The prophet was not martyred. The Salem days had passed. Heresy hunting in the Congregational Church received its quietus. A new day had dawned.

One reviewer said that Bushnell's ideas would "obliterate sectarian division" and that "one generation, trained in the spirit of the view which Dr. Bushnell presents, might banish slavery and war, and many kindred sins." The issues, then, were of great significance.

Horace Bushnell is one of the greatest Christian leaders New England has produced. He is rated among the two or

three ablest preachers and writers, and his influence on
theology has long been recognized. Three biographies of
him have been written and almost innumerable articles and
sketches. But no study has been made of his relation to
religious education. This is all the more remarkable since
his theory of Christian nurture, as stated above, is the
germ idea of all creative education. The relationship is so
obvious as to be almost glaring and yet one may read many
articles and books, and even a recent biography, without
so much as a hint that one of Bushnell's main contributions
was the stimulus and direction he gave to religious education.

The position this study leads to is that Bushnell was
the prophet of this worldwide movement, that some of his
main tenets were basic in its development, and that many
of his very terms and phrases are current in its literature.
Of course, the word prophet does not imply that he
could foretell the future but that he had insight into truth
and grasped its significance for his own day and for the
future.

It is not claimed that Bushnell was the only pioneer.
That would be quite absurd. Such movements do not
spring from any one person, but rather seem to develop
almost spontaneously in many minds and hearts in widely
separated sections of the world. All that is attempted is
to set forth some of his main positions and to suggest their
influence on later developments.

But, in order to show how tremendously significant his
theories were, it is necessary to place them in their original
setting and over against the accepted orthodoxy of the day.
This is comparatively easy because of the controversy they
aroused at the time of publication and the definiteness, not

to say bitterness, with which his critics put themselves on record against him. The sketch here given etches a picture of one aspect of ecclesiastical and orthodox mentality that is characteristic of the times.

A complete study of Bushnell's relation to the religious education movement would include a survey of his revolutionary ideas on Nature and the Supernatural, and on God in Christ (which are the titles of two of his great books). But, except incidentally, such a study is not attempted here. This research limits itself to *Views of Christian Nurture, and of Subjects Adjacent Thereto* published nearly a century ago, in 1847. The plan followed is to show, by examining his previous writings, the genesis of this book; to present rather liberal excerpts from it; and then to quote what leading reviews said about it. A whole chapter is taken up with the attacks of Tyler, which reveal something of the theological background on which the theory of Christian nurture was projected and make his work stand out in high relief. Then the relation of certain outstanding positions of Bushnell to liberal religious ideas today is set forth and the final chapter is an appeal to history after the passing of almost a century.

Two reasons among many for such a study as this may be mentioned. In the first place, religious educators and others should know more about Horace Bushnell as a pioneer and emancipator and especially the prophetic work he did in promoting the education of the people in "the nurture and admonition of the Lord."

In the second place, Bushnell's writings are so fresh and vital that they seem written for today. It is hoped that this book may lead many more to become familiar at least with the selections from his works here reproduced and also read his books more extensively. In addition to those already mentioned, his addresses on the home, on roads, and his classic on "Work and Play" are worthy of being published as tracts for the times.

Bushnell's courage was remarkable. In civic matters he was not afraid to stand alone against powerful political and vested interests. He well knew also that the positions he expounded brought him into serious danger of losing his church and his ministerial standing. Perhaps the reader will see more clearly the significance of the discussions in this book and the significance of Bushnell if some of his main positions are set down briefly. They are as follows:

The child is to grow up a Christian, and never know himself as being otherwise. (See p. 39 and footnote).

He flatly opposed the whole doctrine of total depravity which his opponents held to be axiomatic, unquestionable fact. (See p. 17).

He took a definite stand against revivalism which by many was considered the breath of life to the church.

He opposed highly organized missionary conquest campaigns, advocating instead reliance on the "outpopulating power" of the Christian life.

He advocated Christian nurture as opposed to placing the total emphasis on conversion as the method of promoting Christian living.

He advocated and practiced international and interdenominational fellowship.

He placed great responsibility on parents for the character of their children and the future of civilization, claiming an organic social connection as over against the severe individualism of the time.

He emphasized the teaching ministry of the church, condemning ministers who claimed they were "too busy" to care for children and youth.

He stood strongly for experience in learning, as distinguished from rationalism and the learning of dogma.

These and other positions he took in religious and civic matters, regardless of whether he stood alone (as in clearing up a slum and making the area into a park) or with the majority, as he said himself "neither fearing to make the decision nor making it hastily."

Horace Bushnell's life was also prophetic of the breadth of interest the modern leader in religious education must have. He was no recluse. He loved adventure. As a citizen he threw himself into every movement calculated to promote the welfare of the people. The variety of his interests is amazing, as is indicated in a later chapter (ps. 140-144). Places as far separated as his own city of Hartford and the Pacific Coast retain the impress of his influence. His words inscribed on the west side of the Bushnell Memorial Hall, Hartford, are a reflection of his own life: "Life is always insipid to those who have no great works in hand or no lofty aims to elevate their feelings."

Bushnell was a pioneer. He called himself "One of God's experimenters." He fulfilled the conditions, so necessary to progress, of combining the spirit and objectivity of the scientist with the spiritual glow of the saint. There is always great need for men and women of vision who see beyond the next step and lead the way. He bore the torch.

To him the words of Sir Henry Newbolt apply most fitting-
ly and might be taken as Bushnell's message to all religious
leaders today.

> "This is the word that year by year,
>   While in her place the School is set,
> Everyone of her sons must hear,
>   And none that hears it dare forget.
> This they all with a joyful mind
>   Bear through life like a torch in flame,
> And falling fling to the host behind—
>   'Play up, play up! and play the game!' "

CHAPTER II

THE GENESIS OF THE BOOK "VIEWS OF CHRISTIAN NURTURE"

BUSHNELL'S first publication was a sermon, "Crisis of the Church," printed in 1835. It was against slavery, although he was not an abolitionist.
One of his earliest articles was the review of a book by a phrenologist. The article is entitled, "Influence of Religion upon the Health." [1] It is interesting in several particulars as showing how Bushnell's mind was beginning to work on some of the problems later more fully developed and his scientific attitude to questions of fact.

It is to be noted that he is not swept off his feet by this new "science" of phrenology, though it had a great vogue. At one point he even rebuts it on the theory of chances, showing that, on the most liberal allowances, the chance of truly delineating character from the shape of the head is less than 1 in 2,709,650! (p. 55).

In reply to the author's strictures on the special agency of the Holy Spirit, the reviewer claims that God works in a regular way or according to law but that from the point of view of each individual, whether plant or person, his care

---

[1] *The Quarterly Christian Spectator.* Vol. VIII, 1836. New Haven, Stephen Cooke. Article V, ps. 51-80 (March, 1836), is entitled "Influence of Religion Upon the Health". It is unsigned, but is ascribed to Bushnell by Poole, William Frederick, in *An Index to Periodical Literature*, Boston, James R. Osgood, 1882.

seems special. This idea of law and growth foreshadows somewhat the theory of Christian nurture. He also in a measure defends revivals, which the author of the book apparently ridiculed, but only in so far as they are "sober and intelligent" and not an exhibition of madness and fanaticism, and in so far as they result "in love, meekness, forbearance, charity." (p. 80). But he developed a far more critical attitude in regard to special agency, or what he called the ictic theory, and to revivals, in his later articles and books.

Another article, "Spiritual Economy of Revivals of Religion", appeared in the same magazine in February, 1838.[1] It was republished in *Views of Christian Nurture, and of Subjects Adjacent Thereto,* in 1847, and again, in *Building Eras,* in 1881. It is an interesting foreshadowing of certain points in *Christian Nurture,* which appeared nearly ten years later.

The article opens with this clear statement: "We do not undertake the defense or apology of revivals of religion" and continues, "The term *revival of religion* is one not found in the scriptures, and one to which we have some objections," but, he adds later, "It is of more consequence to measure and guard the term, than to avoid it." (p. 131).

In considering revivals he is led to discuss the doctrine of "spiritual agency," and argues from the variety in nature that similarly there will be great differences in the individu-

---

[1] Vol. X, 1838. New Haven, Hezekiah Howe. Article VIII, ps. 131-148. His daughter, Mrs. Mary Bushnell Cheney, in her *Life and Letters of Horace Bushnell* (New York, Harper & Bros. 1880) mistakenly gives the date as 1836 (p. 82). The footnote in Bushnell's *Building Eras* (N. Y., Scribner's Sons, 1881, p. 150), where the article is reproduced, reads, "First published in the 'Christian Spectator', of 1838, Vol. X."

al experience of religion. But he points out that sometimes "dishonor attaches to the scene of revival itself." (p. 142).

He takes a strong position against the then current emphasis on conversions. To those who say to convert people is the great aim of the church he replies, "As well might it be said, that the great business of travelers is to set out on journeys. The great business of the gospel is to form men to God." (p. 144).

Then he continues with what was really startling: "Let it startle no one, if we declare our conviction, that religion has as deep an interest in the proper conduct of times of non-revival, as in these periods of glowing excitement. For many religious purposes, and those not the least important, a revival is less advantageous than other times. . . . The time, preeminently the time to strengthen principle and consolidate character, is, when there is no public excitement. And for this reason, God's spiritual husbandry includes such times, and makes them so prolonged as to constitute the greater part of life, showing very conclusively the estimate he has of them." (p. 145). That any time could be as important as during a revival was indeed a bold statement to make. He concludes: "Our doctrine naturally terminates here,—in proving it to be the great business and art of the Christian to watch for the mind of the Spirit, and shape the life evermore pliantly thereto." (p. 147).

Another writing of Bushnell's which reveals his style and helped to develop his thinking was his criticism of Bishop Brownell's address. At the annual convention of the Clergy of the Episcopal Diocese of Connecticut, June 13, 1843, Bishop Thomas C. Brownell's charge was entitled

"Errors of the Times." [1] The three errors he discusses are:
the abuses of the right of private judgment; non-episcopal
ordination; and baptism. A reply to this appeared in *The
New Englander*, January, 1844. This article is unsigned,
but the Index (which is marked Volume XX) to the magazine ascribes it to Bushnell, as does Mrs. Cheney. [2] It was
reprinted anonymously in a pamphlet of 51 pages. [3] He is
quite personal, and very critical and ironical. He refers to
"the one little pamphlet with a green cover" emulating the
Oxford Tracts for the Times. (p. 7). [4] He criticises even the
English of the title and hotly resents the continuous references of the Bishop to the members of other denominations
as dissenters. "He well understood that we must receive
as an intended insult the epithet 'dissenters', which he be-
stows upon us, on almost every page of his charge." (p. 9).
Indeed, Bushnell was carried away by the fair sport the
worthy bishop provided especially as to his strictures on
private judgment and non-episcopal ordination. He admits,
however, that the bishop is right "in regard to the disuse,
or little improvement that is made of infant baptism." He

---

[1] The title page reads: *"Errors of the Times.* A charge delivered to
the clergy of the diocese of Connecticut, at the annual convention,
holden in Christ Church, in the city of Hartford, June 13, 1843. Hartford, Case, Tiffany and Co. 1843." It was published in pamphlet form
with green paper cover.

[2] Cheney, Mary Bushnell. *Life and Letters of Horace Bushnell*,
p. 109.

[3] The title page reads as follows: *"Review of the Errors of the
Times.* A charge, by the Rt. Rev. T. C. Brownell, D.D., LL.D. Bishop
of the Diocese of Connecticut: Re-printed from the January Number
of the *New Englander*. Hartford, Edwin Hunt, No. 6 Asylum Street.
1844".

[4] The page references are to the pamphlet.

adds, "Here, for once (and it is the only instance in his charge), he has hit his mark, and we are willing that our churches should see it." (p. 48).

Apparently he was told the review was too severe for, when he republished it in pamphlet form, the last sentence in the introduction is this: "If we are too severe, we are so by a misjudgment, most deliberately formed." (p. 2). But his daughter, Mrs. Cheney, writes that he "afterwards sincerely regretted" the tone of the review "as too harsh in spirit and discourteous in manner."[1]

Still greater progress is made towards a new and constructive statement in an article, "The Kingdom of Heaven as a Grain of Mustard Seed."[2] In it he said: "To roll a snowball and to grow an oak are not the same thing. Enlargement of volume is a result in both cases; but beyond this, they have nothing in common. In one, the result is wrought by an external force; in the other, by a vital force within." (p. 600).

Again he says: "According to the opinion of Christ himself, the church is as a grain of mustard seed, and its future spread is to be as the growth of a tree. It is a creature whose vitality is spiritual life, and it can have its increase only by the same law which pertains in all organic living bodies, i.e. by *development from within, not by external accretion*." (p. 602).

---

[1] Op. cit. p. 109.

[2] *The New Englander Magazine.* Volume II, 1844. B. L. Hamlen. New Haven. October, 1844. ps. 600-619. This is an unsigned article in the magazine, but Bushnell is given as the author in the index volume. He claims it as his own in the preface (p. 4) to his *Views of Christian Nurture, and of Subjects Adjacent Thereto*, under the caption, "Growth, Not Conquest, the True Method of Christian Progress," and republishes it therein under this title. (ps. 147-181).

He had strong views in regard to the way foreign mission work was promoted and carried on. He held that mission work was regarded too much as "a mere society engine fed by money," and as such, it is "truly external to the church." (p. 606). At that time the daily papers were growing rapidly and many expected great religious help from the press, but like an old-time prophet he warns that "To hang any the least expectation on the press, as a substitute for piety, or a piety-saving machine is an egregious delusion." (p. 607).

He pleads for inner spiritual life rather than merely conversions. "If the whole attention of the church is bent to this one object of making conversions, and there is no endeavor to cherish them after they are made; if nothing is valued but conversions, and these are taken as the measure of all good; if revivals of religion are sought, not for the reviving of piety, but for the subjugation of the unbelievers; then is it clear, that the idea of growth is lost in the idea of conquest . . ." (p. 607). The idea of growth "requires every activity to proceed from within. . . . It declares that bustle can not save the world, represses all flippant zeal and forwardness, distinguishes the money giver from the Christian, and warns the church that she is about to perish by the magnitude of her schemes, if she can not sustain them by a proportional measure of holiness and faith in God." (p. 608).

Another point on which Bushnell took a definite stand was in regard to baptism and he now propounds a theory later developed more fully. "We reject the doctrine of baptismal regeneration, as held by Episcopalians. . . . In place of a doctrine so false and pernicious, we hold that children are, in a sense, included in the faith of their parents, partakers with them in their covenant, and brought into a peculiar relation to God, in virtue of it. . . . As to the precise time or manner in which they are to receive the germ of holy principle, nothing is affirmed." (p. 610). . . . The following statement comes close to his central principle in *Christian Nurture*: "The Moravians too have very nearly realized our doctrine. As many as nine out of ten in that most interesting church, we are assured, have no conception of a time when they entered on the Christian life." (p. 611).

If the child is not able to grow up in God he points out the dilemma that inevitably results and that no theologian who held the mediæval view could ever resolve. "If it may not grow up in holy virtue,—if it must grow up in sin, till it comes to some definite age, before it is a candidate for repentance and a new life, then, during that interval, is it seen to lie under a doom more dismal and hapless than any other we are acquainted with in this world. Capable of sin—incapable of repentance! . . . Might not the church better say, in her Savior's name, 'Of such is the kingdom of heaven,' and clasp it to her arms.

"If our views on this head are admitted,—if it is God's design in the household covenant, that the children shall grow up to be Christians, and this result may and ought to be realized, then, most clearly, is it seen that there is a law of spiritual population in the church, analogous to the law of physical population in states." (p. 612).

But he adds that the greatest resource and glory of the church which gives her power of growth is "her own internal life—the life of God." (p. 615).

The prevailing emphasis on depravity and the need of conversion not only loses the children to the church "which is too great a loss" (p. 617), but also prevents the highest development. "One principal reason why we are so often deficient in character, or outward beauty, is, that piety begins so late in life, having thus to maintain a perpetual and unequal war with previous habit. . . . (p. 617).

"We thrust our children out of the covenant first," he says and "Then we go out, at least on certain occasions, to convert them back, as if they themselves were heathens." By the emphasis on "a certain abrupt technical experience", the idea of "Accretion displaces growth." (ps. 617-618).

In this same article he says: "Here too is the greatest impediment to a true missionary spirit. The habit of conquest runs to dissipation and irregularity. . . . Whereas, if the church were unfolding the riches of the covenant at her firesides and tables—if the children were identified with religion from the first, and grew up in Christian love of man, the missionary spirit would not throw itself up in irregular jets, but would flow as a river. And so much is there in this, that we do not believe it possible to produce a steady, patient, practical spirit of missions, except through the education of childhood." (p. 618).

His words to parents are thrilling and are as timely today as when written: "We ask then of every parent, that he will seriously review his impressions on this subject. . . . Let family religion be a domestic miniature of heaven, not a dull formality. Let him be there, as the gardener among his opening flowers, expecting their fragrance and beauty, not that they will all be thistles—expecting it, because God hath promised, and the dews of his grace are perpetually felt." (ps. 618-619). He not only preached but practiced this faith and his letters to his children reveal that it was the atmosphere of the Bushnell home. [1]

His sermon on "Unconscious Influence", 1845 [2] dwells on some of the germ ideas later expanded in the published volume. He insists on the enormous power of one's daily life, urging that the involuntary influence is as great as the voluntary, conscious teaching of Christianity. Ever mindful of the supreme importance of the character development of children, he shows how unconscious influence operates through their imitation and later through their respect for others and the quick enthusiasms which kindle and spread among youth. He hit upon the idea that goodness is infectious and propagates itself. This idea he developed more fully in relation to missions. He pleads for propagation over against what he claimed was the policy of conquest, in this also taking an independent position in direct conflict with many who, under the enthusiasm of great missionary campaigns, thought too much of organization, raising money, and making converts.

It is difficult to imagine what a stir these writings made. They took sharp issue at several points with the New England theology and church practices. The sharp contrast is not appreciated today because now so many churches accept the positions he then advocated.

Dr. Bushnell took a trip to Europe in 1845, soon after the last article appeared, and when he returned he was

---

[1] Cheney, Mary Bushnell, *Life and Letters of Horace Bushnell.* ps. 140-142; 188-190.

[2] Included in the volume *Sermons for the New Life,* New York, Scribner, 1859. This discourse was selected by Grenville Kleiser as one of the "World's Great Sermons".

asked by the ministerial association to which he belonged
to present the matter more fully there. In response to
this request he read two sermons evidently prepared for
the regular services in his own church. The ministers considered them so important that they asked him to have them
published, making only a few suggestions as to changes in
certain phrases.

Through the Reverend Joseph H. Towne of Boston, a
life member of the Massachusetts Sabbath School Society
and a member of the Committee of Publication, the manuscript without any name attached, was presented to the
publication committee. So, as Bushnell said, "It made its
first impression as anonymous." [1] Convinced for themselves
of its worth, they feared what effect it might have on the
public and on their own society. "Mr. Towne described,
in a graphic letter to Dr. Bushnell, the manner in which
the committee received and discussed the anonymous manuscript. Each member of the committee, as he read and
reported upon it, agreed to it as true, and praised it as
'valuable,' 'no common production,' 'highly suggestive.'
'But,' the qualification was, 'it is new; it will make a stir;
some persons will be startled by it,—such is the novelty of
the thing that it will inevitably draw attention to itself

---

[1] Bushnell, Horace. *An Argument for "Discourses on Christian
Nurture"*, addressed to the Publishing Committee of the Massachusetts
Sabbath School Society. Hartford, Edwin Hunt, No. 6 Asylum Street,
1847. p. 3.

This has led Dr. George Stewart in his very thorough *History of
Religious Education in Connecticut to the Middle of the Nineteenth
Century*, to make a slight error, saying that the "Massachusetts Sabbath School Society published it anonymously". p. 351 (New Haven,
Yale University Press, 1924). The manuscript made its first appeal
to the committee anonymously but it was published under Bushnell's
name. The title page, reproduced by Dr. Stewart (p. 349), shows this.

whenever it appears in print. Would it be prudent to publish it?' After reserving their decision for several months, during which time the propriety of publishing it was thoroughly considered, and after sending the manuscript back twice to the author for the modification of phrases, in which, as it cost him no change of opinion, he was willing to gratify the committee, the 'Discourses on Christian Nurture' was finally published," [1] making a tiny volume of 72 small pages (6¼ x 4 inches). This is the title page:

DISCOURSES
ON
CHRISTIAN NURTURE

BY HORACE BUSHNELL
PASTOR OF THE NORTH CHURCH, HARTFORD

Approved by the Committee of Publication
BOSTON:
MASSACHUSETTS SABBATH SCHOOL SOCIETY
1847 [2]

The little book was well received. Bushnell says, "Some little commendatory notices appeared. The most strongly Calvinistic, and as many judge, the most thoroughly respectable Congregational paper in New England (precisely what I should have expected), was full and decided in its commendation, and published extracts, I have

---

[1] Cheney, Mary Bushnell, op. cit. p. 179.

[2] Mrs. Cheney and, probably following her, Dr. Edwin Pond Parker give the date as 1846. Dr. Theodore T. Munger gives the date as 1846 in the text (p. 67) though he has it 1847 in the list of "Published Writings" (p. xi).

been told, for the benefit of its readers. It was noticed with qualified favor (which also I should have expected), by a very candid and highly respected writer in the Episcopal paper of this city. It seemed about to get audience, in fact, before the public, without producing any alarm whatever." [1]

But then the attack began. Dr. Bennet Tyler was president of the Theological Institute of Connecticut at East Windsor. This theological school had been founded in 1834 to controvert what was regarded as the unsound teaching of the Divinity School in New Haven. This doubtless made Dr. Tyler feel himself the defender of the faith and spokesman for orthodoxy.

Besides, Dr. Tyler had published a book entitled, *New England Revivals as They Existed at the Close of the Eighteenth and the Beginning of the Nineteenth Centuries,* in 1845, gathering his information especially from the *Connecticut Evangelical Magazine.* It is difficult to realize now how great was the emphasis on revivals and conversions. Each year in the denominational meetings a regular standing committee always reviewed the state of religion in the church and this was usually little more than a report of revivals and the number of conversions during the year. Even in the Sunday schools the emphasis was often on conversions and revivals.

Besides all this, it was a time when the theological lines were strictly drawn and especially so between Hartford and New Haven, for what was called the Tyler-Taylor controversy was raging. Ministers grouped themselves on either side. For example, Rev. Dr. Edwin Pond Parker

---

[1] Bushnell, Horace. *An Argument for "Discourses on Christian Nurture".* p. 4.

said, "In all that controversy as between East Windsor and New Haven, between Tylerism and Taylorism, the following ministers,—Joel Hawes, Noah Porter, Oliver E. Daggett, Horace Bushnell, and Rev. Mr. Spring of East Hartford, were on the New Haven and Taylor side, and, strange as it may now seem, were regarded by many as defective in theology." [1] Naturally enough, perhaps, Dr. Tyler would be especially displeased at any one in the vicinity of his new institution who was on the New Haven side.

Then finally, Tyler's and Bushnell's types of mind were antipathetic. Bushnell's was expansive, grasping wholes, venturesome, careless of picayune details; while Tyler was the opposite. For him, to be safe and orthodox seemed most desirable in a minister.

With these things in mind, it is evident that Bushnell's articles almost ruling out revivals, substituting nurture, and blazing new trails must have been bombshells and that Tyler should feel called upon to defend the faith. How thoroughly he tried to shatter Bushnell, both by writing and by ecclesiastical action, will appear in the sequel.

His first move was to read a criticism of the *Discourses on Christian Nurture* before the North Association of Hartford County very soon after its appearance. This criticism was immediately issued in pamphlet form as a letter to Dr. Bushnell, and is dated East Windsor, June 7, 1847. The reason for its publication as stated in the postscript is because "The brethren expressed their *unanimous* approba-

---

[1] Parker, Edwin Pond, D.D. *The Hartford Central Association and The Bushnell Controversy.* An Historical address given before The Hartford Central Association, February 3, 1896. Published by the Association, Hartford, The Case, Lockwood and Brainard Co. press. p. 6.

tion of it, and requested that it might be published." [1] Later Tyler published seven other letters on this controversy, and all eight will be considered in Chapter IV.

The Christian Observatory [2] of July, 1847, contains a review of the *Discourses on Christian Nurture,* which opens with these rather ominous words: "In the year of our Lord 1651, the Great and General Court imposed a heavy fine upon a clergyman of Massachusetts, for 'letting fall sundry weak, unsafe, unsound, and inconvenient expressions in his public teaching and ministry. . . .' And if our admired friend, the author of these discourses had fallen on their times, we fear that the state-physicians who watched over the health and soundness of the body-politic, would have bled him, with their mulcts and fines, in the 'pocket vein', even to fainting." (p. 323).

But he has a certain admiration for his foolhardy and spectacular stunts. "We feel a hearty sympathy with the bold and independent turn of Dr. Bushnell's mind, except when it runs out into a sort of reckless daring; like that of the climbers of mast-heads and pinnacles, who crave the excitement of needless danger, and exult in blanching the cheeks of the trembling spectators of their giddy feats. . . ." (p. 323) and adds, ". . . we have sighed to think that he could not be regarded as what judicious old Christians used to call 'a safe man.'" (p. 324). What a compliment this is in the light of history that he was not "safe" in the sense intended.

---

[1] Tyler, Bennet, D.D. *Letter to Dr. Bushnell on "Christian Nurture".* East Windsor Hill, June 7, 1847. p. 22.

[2] A. W. McClure, editor. Volume I, 1847. Boston, published by J. V. Beane and Co. July, 1847. ps. 323-330.

Then he casts reflections on the common honesty of Bushnell. "In entering upon the 'Discourses on Christian Nurture', we stumble at the very threshold. The book professes, in the 'Advertisement', to be published at the request of an association of ministers before whom it was read. Whereas, if we are rightly informed, no vote to that effect was passed." (ps. 324-325).

This was a gratuitous insult. "The "Advertisement" did not claim that a vote had been taken, but merely that it "was read before an Association of ministers, who requested their publication." Bushnell was naturally stung by the expression, and replied in the *Argument for "Discourses on Christian Nurture"*: "I do not recollect that any one seriously objected to the view given, or desired any correction more radical than the addition of some verbal qualifications. A venerable father, whose name is a name of confidence and respect, second to no other in our churches, offered a motion that I should be requested to print the discourses. No one objected, and the vote was passed, I believe, *nem con.* They were not produced for publication, but my strong conviction of the importance of the subject and of the view presented, induced me afterwards to comply." [1] A writer in the *New-England Religious Herald* [2] of August 7, 1847, referring to Tyler's statement said: "Some of the reviewers of the 'Christian Nurture', report that Dr. Bushnell was not requested to publish it. This is a mistake. The Central Association of this County did, to our knowledge, pass a vote asking him to publish it."

---

[1] *An Argument for "Discourses on Christian Nurture"*. p. 3.

[2] Originally *The Religious Herald*. A Hartford weekly paper. Vol. V. August 7, 1847. Each issue is paged separately.

Then the reviewer comes out with the explicit statement placing his positions clearly in opposition to Bushnell's and revealing how fearfully archaic those positions,
as he held them, are today: "It is the grand defect in Dr.
Bushnell's scheme, that it does not properly recognize the
truths of depravity and regeneration, and cannot easily harmonize with them. These doctrines we *know* to be true,
whatever we may think of his book." He is scandalized
that anything like "goodness" might be supposed to be "dormant" in the mind of a child, "and only needed to be roused
by some happy touch." [1] (p. 325).

He pours scorn on Bushnell's theory of "something like
a law of organic connection as regards character subsisting
between them" (parent and child). One of the weaknesses, he says, is that "It teaches that man, as to his body,
is viviparous; and as to his soul, is oviparous." (ps. 327-
328).

He is quite incensed that Bushnell should use the German people as an example of anything good. His lurid
criticism reveals his own breadth of view! He says: "The
mass of them (the Germans) is ruined by vain philosophy,
and corrupted by dead rationalism and ghostly transcen-
dentalism, and all those hard and hateful names which
designate the numerous shapes of Christian Infidelity which
have swarmed from the fumes of their beer and tobacco,
like the locusts from the smoke of the bottomless pit. . . . It
is really mortifying to see the pastor of a flock of Connecticut saints, leading them out of their fat valley into
such lean and unwholesome pasture." (p. 329). His righteous soul is hurt for this wounding of "Connecticut saints."

---

[1] *The Christian Observatory*, July, 1847.

This kind of appeal to the galleries is characteristic of the Tyler type of mind.   In another place, it is shown how careful Bushnell was in his statement in reference to the Germans, and how obviously he was misinterpreted and misrepresented. [1]

The reviewer is very much concerned about one thing. If parents are encouraged to feel that their children may "grow up Christians" will not "every child who feels that he has been piously trained by parents whose religious character he venerates, be apt to conclude that he has grown up accordingly?" (ps. 329-330).   This would, he believes, be a grave danger!   In conclusion, however, he commends quite heartily the section in Bushnell on the duty of parents to their children.

In the next number of this same magazine [2] there is a note on Tyler's letter to Bushnell, which contains this very interesting comment: "This pamphlet, called out by the 'Discourses on Christian Nurture', is written both ably and kindly.   While it breathes an amiable (!) spirit toward Dr. Bushnell, it makes shocking bad work of the theology of his little book.   The cask is overset and emptied, the heads stove in, the hoops knocked off, and the staves flung all over the lot.   That cask must be hard to mend.   It will be easier to make a new one."   (ps. 381-382).

To this a writer in *The Christian Mirror* [3] replied: "Our good Boston brother must have been suffering some optical illusion, when he saw the Dr.'s cask demolished, and

---

[1] *An Argument for "Discourses on Christian Nurture".* p. 31.

[2] *The Christian Observatory, A Religious and Literary Magazine.* Volume I, 1847.   August, 1847.   ps. 381-383.

[3] Quoted in *The New-England Religious Herald*, August 28, 1847.

the 'staves scattered all round the lot.' It is still entire, well headed, soundly hooped, and capable of bearing, unharmed, harder knocks than have yet been dealt to it."

The critic did not say what "the cask" contained. But looking back in the light of nearly a century, his exuberance is hardly justified. Its central thesis of Christian nurture is now generally accepted, while Tyler's type of mind and of theology are both thoroughly discredited. The cask apparently was full of dynamite, which Dr. Tyler, by calling attention to it so violently, helped to explode. Its force is still great; but where is the exploder!

This reviewer then quotes from other reviewers: "A writer in Pennsylvania, believed to be Dr. Nevin, a decided enemy of Puritanism, says, in a review of the work: 'The current view of Christian Nurture, as *opposed* by Dr. Bushnell, has been the product to a great extent undoubtedly, of the Puritan theory of religion.' No wonder, then, if Rationalist speculators should be distractedly in love with their Hartford friend." (p. 382).

He also delights in reporting various Unitarians who agreed with certain things in Bushnell. The writer belongs to that type who seek to blast an idea to which they are opposed by tagging it with a name, such as Rationalist or Unitarian, in disfavor at the time in his group. He bemoans the fact that "he (Bushnell) virtually abolishes the dogmas of Total Depravity, Election, Instantaneously Completed Conversion." (p. 382) . . . . It is interesting that now the religious world has little use for any of these doctrines as then stated and understood.

The results of Tyler's letter and the agitation it started led the Massachusetts Sabbath School Society to withdraw the book, almost immediately. This could be considered nothing but weak-kneed, remembering that the committee themselves heartily approved the positions taken, as is shown by Towne's letter.

The sudden surrender of the committee and the ignominy of having the book withdrawn naturally stung Dr. Bushnell, and he published a slashing defence in pamphlet form entitled, *An Argument for "Discourses on Christian Nurture"*, addressed to the Publishing Committee of the Massachusetts Sabbath School Society. [1] The "Argument" is in somewhat the same spirit as his review of Dr. Brownell's charge. It is distinctly an earlier manner which he later deliberately gave up. At his twentieth anniversary as minister of the North Church of Hartford, he said in an address: [2] "Regretting some things which I had heretofore published, not as unjust to others, but as too violent in the manner to be just to myself and the meekness of the Christian spirit, I had determined, from the first, to have no controversy over these discourses, a determination to which I have resolutely adhered, though perceiving, every day, the advantage taken of my silence." (ps. 23-24).

The stir caused no small demand for the book; so, as Bushnell had reserved his rights to the manuscript, he published it himself that same year, under the title, *Views of Christian Nurture, and of Subjects Adjacent Thereto*. Edwin Hunt, the Hartford publisher, had this advertisement in *The New England Religious Herald* of October 30, 1847: "This day published Dr. Bushnell's celebrated work on Christian Nurture, which has so long been suppressed

---

[1] Hartford, Edwin Hunt, 1847.
[2] Bushnell, Horace. *Twentieth Anniversary.* A Commemorative Discourse, delivered in the North Church, of Hartford, May 22, 1853. Hartford, Elihu Geer, Stationer and Printer, 10 State St. MDCCCLIII. 32 ps.

by the Massachusetts Sabbath School Society; together
with other subjects adjacent thereto, expressive of his
views on the Spiritual Economy of Revivals and of the
duties of Churches and Church Members, etc. October 28.
Edwin Hunt, 6 Asylum St."

This edition included the two original discourses, the
argument, two republished articles,—"Spiritual Economy
of Revivals of Religion" and "Growth, Not Conquest, the
True Method of Christian Progress,"—and two additional
sermons, "Organic Unity of the Family" and "The Scene
of the Pentecost, and a Christian Parish," which made a
closely printed volume of 251 pages.

It was the controversy which Tyler started that
brought the matter so prominently before the whole country, for, as *The Christian Observatory*, a strongly anti-
Bushnell journal, pointed out in a later edition, [1] "That
which began in a retired ministerial circle in Connecticut;
and which, in little more than a year, has become a controversy of widely extended interest, will continue to en-
gage the attention of the ministry and the churches." The
writer spoke more truly than he knew, though the outcome
has been the opposite of what he predicted and so fondly
hoped.

The attacks brought the issue clearly to the fore.
Bushnell near the end of his preface writes these brave
words: "Not concealing the importance of the question
we have now on hand, let us handle it earnestly, neither
fearing to make the decision, nor making it hastily." [2] Perhaps few, if any, saw as clearly as he that "the question is

---

[1] Volume II, June, 1848. p. 283.
[2] *Views of Christian Nurture, and of Subjects Adjacent Thereto.*
p. 4.

one that involves, in one way or another, all the most abstruse points in theology"; and also "one moreover that concerns a child, a very peculiar being, whose internal history is the darker, that it does not lie within the scope of adult consciousness and experience. Therefore," he concludes the preface, "my readers will need to have some patience with themselves, and it will not be wrong if they extend some degree of patience to me."

Now the controversy is boiling. Tyler issued seven more letters in a numbered series;[1] and long reviews appeared in leading magazines. Two years later (1849) Bushnell published *God in Christ*. All the fury of those who considered him not "safe" and his writings full of "dangerous tendencies" broke out with greater intensity.

Tyler's opposition was by no means confined to writing letters. An ecclesiastic of his type, as the whole range of history shows, has other weapons even more deadly. He was not slow to use them. When Bushnell's *God in Christ* was published in 1849, there were accusations of heresy. The Rev. Amos S. Chesebrough, a contemporary and friend, is doubtless quite correct in saying that there was a concerted plan to crush Bushnell, for this is corroborated by other lines of evidence. It is best to quote his statement rather fully. "It seemed as if the systematic onset upon the book was the result of a concerted plan to crush out the errors in it by one strong combined effort, and that for this end each theological center was to furnish a champion. The first of these criticisms came from the Divinity School

---

[1] Tyler, Bennet, D.D. *Letters to the Rev. Horace Bushnell, D.D.* containing Strictures on his book entitled *Views of Christian Nurture, and of Subjects Adjacent Thereto.* Hartford, Brown and Parsons, 1848.

at New Haven. Under the caption "What Does Dr. Bushnell mean?" three articles signed "Omicron", appeared in
The New York Evangelist, which were gathered into a
pamphlet of twenty-eight pages and extensively distributed.
In the course of a week or two Princeton Seminary gave
its weighty verdict in an article of forty pages in *The Biblical Repertory and Princeton Review.* The next assault was
made by *The Christian Observatory,* a religious monthly
edited by seven leading Congregational ministers of Boston,
in an article of sixty pages, bitter in the extreme. About
the same time there emanated from Bangor Theological
Seminary a volume of one hundred and eighteen pages, entitled, *A Review of Dr. Bushnell's "God in Christ".* The
Theological Seminary at East Windsor furnished no formal
review, but kept up a running fire on the book in the
columns of *The Religious Herald,* a Hartford weekly. There
were other reviews and critical notices, but these were the
leading ones, and enough of them to have demolished a full
score of heretics. [1]

Chesebrough himself, under the pen name of Criticus
Criticorum, did a very clever piece of work. In a series
of articles in *The New-England Religious Herald* he ana-
lyzed the critics' reviews, showing their radical disagree-
ment with each other, which was quite devastating. The
articles had to be discontinued, but the material was all
published as a pamphlet entitled, *Contributions of CC., Now
Declared in Full as Criticus Criticorum.* [2]

---

[1] *Bushnell Centenary.* Minutes of the General Association of Connecticut at the One Hundred and Ninety-third Annual Meeting held
in Hartford, June 17, 18, 1902. Hartford Press. The Case, Lockwood
and Brainard Co., 1902. (p. 50) "Reminiscences of the Bushnell Controversy", by Amos S. Chesebrough.

[2] Chesebrough, Amos S. (Published by request) Hartford, Brown
and Parsons, 1849.

The other weapon was ecclesiastical machinery and a heresy trial. The Tyler influence was one of the moving forces in this, and no pains were spared that astute ecclesiastics could concoct and bulldog determination carry out.

The following sketch of this attack is taken from the *Appeal of the Association of Fairfield West to the Associated Ministers connected with The General Association of Connecticut,*[1] a document of 95 pages. This is supplemented with an address by Dr. Edwin Pond Parker which was given at the Hartford Central Association on February 3, 1896 and was published by the Association in pamphlet form.[2]

As Dr. Parker was also a minister in Hartford and had been all through the fight himself his brief sketch is undoubtedly accurate.

The first move was made in 1849 to bring him to trial before the Consociation of which he was a member and the matter was referred to a committee. This committee voted seventeen to three against bringing him to trial, and even the three had reservations. The Fairfield West Association about the same time memorialized the General Association, but its judgment was that such matters pertained to the District Associations. Then Fairfield West in a long document urged the Hartford Central Association to reconsider the case, which they refused to do, giving reasons in writing. The Fairfield West Association then printed its remonstrances and complaint, a pamphlet of thirty pages, which it circulated "to each District Association (excepting

---

[3] New York. Printed for the Association of Fairfield West, by Baker, Godwin & Company, 1852.

[4] *The Hartford Central Association and the Bushnell Controversy.* Hartford, 1896. 29 p.

Hartford Central)". Hartford North, not content with this, broadcast its reply in three religious journals, insuring damaging publicity. Dr. Tyler wrote Hartford Central, but received only an official reply, saying that after fair examination they had found no cause for trial. Fairfield West then memorialized the General Association, asking that Hartford Central be compelled to take some action. The General Association pronounced that it was the duty of the District Association to consider such a remonstrance but refused to violate their constitution. But Fairfield West was not yet through. Again it petitioned Hartford Central to act. Its "communication so abundant in offensive imputations provoked some feeling of resentment in the minds of our brethren." (p. 17). Again this Association sent a judicial reply refusing to reopen the case. Fairfield West compiled a document of nearly one hundred printed pages, which was distributed throughout the state over the protest of nine of the ministers present. Dr. Tyler's motion declaring that it proved Bushnell denied fundamental doctrines of the Christian religion was carried in the Hartford North Association. They forced the matter before the General Association which again ruled that it was not a judicial body.

Another move was possible. If three members of his own congregation "could be found to sign articles of impeachment" he might have been brought before the Consociation for trial. But in spite of all the efforts that had been made, this was never done. It is a remarkable tribute to Dr. Bushnell and to his church that no three of a large congregation would take that step. Annoyed by the whole persecution, his church decided to withdraw from the Consociation, and soon after the Consociation itself disappeared. The congregation proved itself well worthy of Dr. Bushnell's tribute to them on his twentieth anniversary. [1] "These three were not to be found among you, or any one of them. The commotion without had raised no commotion with you. Many looked on with wonder, as upon a besieged city, to see you unshaken, stedfast still in your confidence, ruffled by no concern, and not even so much as moved to break silence. Had you done even this, it would have comforted my accusers, and weakened the dignity both of your position and of mine. And the secret of all this, if it must be told, is that God was with us, and that no position is weak that is sheltered by the peace of God." (p. 23)

Fairfield West then secretly prepared a case addressed to the General Association, signed by fifty-one ministers asking that because of its failure to act in the Bushnell case, the Hartford Central Association be cut off from its fellowship in the General Association. This failed. Resolutions to advise Hartford Central to proceed to trial were defeated. Their last gun was fired in 1854 when they tried to get a resolution through the General Assembly "that they would no longer vouch for the orthodoxy of any minister or Association in virtue of its good standing in the General Association, but would exercise judgment for themselves in every case." Dr. Parker continues, [2] 'The disrespectful temper and schismatical tenor of this document provoked general indignation, and but for Dr. Bushnell it might have been tabled for effrontery. Its only good effects

---

[1] *Twentieth Anniversary.* A Commemorative Discourse.

[2] The Hartford Central Association and the Bushnell Controversy. p. 23.

were a disclosure of the complete breakdown of the campaign, and the great speech by Dr. Bushnell which it called forth."

The whole heresy hunt apparently brought one result. The Congregational churches in New England lost any taste they may have had for this sort of thing.   Heresy hunting was a dead issue.

Bushnell published a greatly enlarged edition of *Christian Nurture* in 1861. [1] The first two chapters are the two original discourses. Of them the author says in the preface, "I could not easily consent to lay aside, or pass into oblivion, the two discourses above referred to; for, under the fortune that befel them, they had become a little historical." (p. v). He also included the address on the organic unity of the family. He continues: "Thirteen new essays, in the form of discourses, though never used as such, but written simply for the discussion's sake, are thus added; and the volume, which virtually covers the ground of a treatise, takes the form of successive topical discussions, or essays, on so many themes, included in the general subject." (p. 41). The volume is thus practically new.

After Bushnell's death and the bitterness of the controversy had passed away, the significance of his theories began to be more fully realized and they had a great influence in shaping thought in relation to religious education. The new movement in this field embodied very largely his views. It is the virility of his ideas and language which accounts for new editions of *Christian Nurture* being called for in 1912, and again in 1916. [2]

---

[1] Charles Scribner's Sons, New York, 1861.
[2] Charles Scribner's Sons, New York.

The following three chapters will show Bushnell's positions and the criticisms made. The final chapters will indicate something of how Bushnell's ideas influenced others and are in broad outline incorporated in the thinking of today, though, of course, it is not pretended that this has come about as the direct result of his work alone. That one should anticipate in his thinking important positions arrived at by progressive leaders a century later, especially a century remarkable for most rapid and fundamental changes in almost every area of human interest, is in itself a remarkable achievement.

CHAPTER III

WHAT THE REVIEWS SAID ABOUT "VIEWS OF CHRISTIAN NURTURE"

T HE MASSACHUSETTS SABBATH SCHOOL SOCIETY, as has been seen, withdrew Bushnell's little book *Discourses on Christian Nurture* and he issued a greatly enlarged edition entitled *Views of Christian Nurture, and of Subjects Adjacent Thereto* [1] in the same year. Because of the publicity already received and the worth of the book itself the leading religious magazines devoted considerable space to it in their reviews. All references, in these reviews quoted here are, then, to this new edition.

The review in *The Christian Observatory* of July, 1847 has already been commented on (ps. 15-19). It had an ominous opening, referred to Bushnell's "reckless daring," and contained a gratuitous insult, questioning whether he was ever asked to publish the discourses. It was undoubtedly by Tyler, whose severe letters will be considered later.

The main criticisms in this review, as already pointed out, were that Bushnell's scheme does not properly recognize "the truths of depravity and regeneration" which Tyler dogmatically declares "we *know* to be true"; asserts that some "goodness" might be dormant in the mind of a child which "only needed to be roused by some happy touch"; that "something like a law of organic connection" exists between parent and child; that the German people should

---

[1] Hartford. Edwin Hunt, No. 6 Asylum Street, 1847. 251 p.

be used as an example of anything good (to the wounding of his "Connecticut saints"!) ; and that children may grow up Christians. He does, however, commend the section on the duty of parents to their children.

There were nine other extensive reviews, which will be considered in this chapter. And in those days book reviews were serious things. Some of these comprise thirty to forty magazine pages of small type!

In the August number of *The Christian Observatory* [1] (referred to above) the writer reports that the editor of *The World* of July 3, 1847, a Unitarian paper, "makes a serious proposition to purchase from the Massachusetts Sabbath School Society, the copy-right of the work, and the balance of the first edition; promises to sell the future editions at half the cost of this; and offers to print a reasonable amount of explanation by way of preface, if the Committee of Publication 'shall feel anxious to explain the reasons which have induced them to part with so *extraordinary* and dangerous a production.'—A work thus reprobated by a large part of the evangelical community, and thus welcomed by the whole body of the Unitarians of all sorts, can hardly be thought a *safe* book for orthodox Sabbath Schools. Accordingly the Publishing Committee of the Massachusetts Society, in deference to the views of their brethren, have voted to suspend the sale of the work."

His enemies used this against Bushnell. If the Unitarians were in favor of the book, it must be wrong. Again history shows that foresight, good judgment, and light may come from unexpected quarters, even from Unitarians and other "sects"!

---

[1] Volume I, August, 1847. ps. 382-383.

The New Englander Magazine reviews the history of the Massachusetts Sabbath School Society's act up to the time of publication and then adds:[1] "When it came out, the Committee might well have been surprised that it was so well received. All sorts of Christians seem to have been delighted, not merely with the integrity and perfection of the thing, but with its future promise.

"On a sudden, a letter is written from Connecticut, which suggests certain 'dangerous tendencies' as lying concealed in the discourses, and expresses surprise that the Committee of the Massachusetts Sabbath School Society had not observed them.

"*Post hoc* (whether *propter hoc*, the committee themselves best know), the book disappears from the market."

A most important and weighty review came from Dr. Charles Hodge of Princeton,[2] who was one of the leading exponents of Calvinism, and Bushnell's enemies expected a shattering analysis from him. But they must have been grievously disappointed. He is very fair, dwelling on the main issues and so is a sharp contrast to Tyler, both

---

[1] Volume 5, January-October, 1847, New Haven. Published by A. H. Maltby, printed by B. L. Hamlen, printer to Yale College. "The New Theological Controversy", October, 1847. ps. 613-614.

[2] *The Biblical Repertory and Princeton Review.* January-October, 1847. Philadelphia: M. B. Hope; John T. Robinson, Printer, Princeton. "Bushnell on Christian Nurture", October, ps. 502-539. Ascribed to Professor Charles Hodge in the Index Volume to the magazine (1825-1868) p. 210; and by Theodore T. Munger, in his book, *Horace Bushnell, Preacher and Theologian.* Boston and New York, Houghton, Mifflin and Company, 1899. p. 82, footnote.

This article was later published in pamphlet form under the title: "Review of Dr. Bushnell's Discourses on Christian Nurture", extracted, by permission, from *The Princeton Review.* New York: Leavitt, Trow & Co. 1847.

in spirit and method. Indeed, his whole review is remarkably favorable. Considering the fact that the book has been withdrawn from publication his words are even more significant and they are timely today: "We cannot regret that the book has seen the light, and done, or at least begun, its work. We anticipate immeasurably more good than evil from its publication. What is wrong, we trust will be sifted out and perish, what is right, will live and operate." (p. 504). His reasons for these statements are given and are worthy of being repeated for their own sake as well as for the light they throw on the controversy: "First, the fact that there is such a divinely constituted relation between the piety of parents and that of their children, as to lay a scriptural foundation for a confident expectation, in the use of the appointed means, that the children of believers will become truly the children of God. We do not like the form in which Dr. Bushnell states this fact; much less, as we shall probably state more fully in the sequel, the mode in which he accounts for it, but the fact itself is most true and precious. It is founded on the express and repeated declaration and promise of God. (p. 504).

" . . . There is an intimate and divinely established connexion between the faith of parents and the salvation of their children; such a connexion as authorizes them to plead God's promises, and to expect with confidence, that through his blessing on their faithful efforts, their children will grow up the children of God. This is the truth and the great truth, which Dr. Bushnell asserts. This doctrine it is his principal object to establish. It is this that gives his book its chief value. This and its consequences render his discourses so appropriate to the present state of the church; for there is perhaps no one doctrine to which it is

more important in our day to call the attention of the
people of God. (p. 509).

"A second truth prominently presented by our author
is that parental nurture, or Christian training, is the great
means for the salvation of the children of the church. We
of course recognize the native depravity of children. . . .
But what we think is plainly taught in scripture, what is
reasonable in itself, and confirmed by the experience of the
church is, that early, assiduous and faithful religious culture of the young, especially by believing parents, is the
great means of their salvation. . . . The child is sedulously
guarded as far as possible from all corrupting influence,
and subjected to those which tend to lead him to God. . . .
When he comes to maturity, the nature of the covenant of
grace is fully explained to him, he intelligently and deliberately assents to it, publicly confesses himself to be a wor-
shipper and follower of Christ, and acts consistently with
his engagements. This is no fancy sketch. Such an experience is not uncommon in actual life." (ps. 509-510).
This is a direct contradiction of one of Tyler's scathing
criticisms which appeared in his first letter, published in
June of this year and which is quoted on pages 52-53.

Dr. Hodge continues: "Success in the use of this
means is the very thing promised to parents in the covenant
into which they are commanded to introduce their children.
. . . How much greater, humanly speaking, is the advantage
which a parent possesses than any preacher can have, in
his constant intercourse with his child, in his hold on its
confidence and love, and in the susceptibility to good impressions which belongs to the early period of life. . . . In
no part of his Discourses nor in his Argument in their
defence, is Dr. Bushnell so true or eloquent as in what he

says of the natural power of parental influence, even before the development of reason in the child." (ps. 510-511).

Dr. Hodge goes on to show that this was the faith and practice of the church. "In the early church, the instruction of the young was made a principal part of parental and ministerial duty. When religion began to decline, and men were taught that baptism wrought the change which God had appointed Christian nurture to effect, then religious education was neglected, and ritualism supplanted piety. When the gospel was revived, Christian nurture revived with it." (p. 513).

He even agrees very largely with Bushnell in regard to the overemphasis on revivals which must have been another sore disappointment to Dr. Tyler. "We shall not, it is hoped, be suspected of denying or of undervaluing the importance either of the public preaching of the gospel, or of revivals of religion. . . .What however we no less believe, and feel constrained in conscience to say is, that a great and hurtful error has taken fast hold on the mind of the church on this subject. Many seem to regard these extraordinary seasons as the only means of promoting religion. So that if these fail, everything fails. Others again, if they do not regard them as the only means for that end, still look upon them as the greatest and the best. They seem to regard this alternation of decline and revival as the normal condition of the church; as that which God intended and which we must look for; that the cause of Christ is to advance not by a growth analogous to the progress of spiritual life in the individual believer, but by sudden and violent paroxysms of exertion. We do not believe this, because it is out of analogy with all God's dealings with men. Life in no form is thus fitful. . . . These revivals are in a great measure, if we may so speak, an idiosyncrasy of our country. They are called *American* revivals. There is nothing American however in true religion. It is the same in its nature, and in its means of progress in all parts of the world. . . . (ps. 519-520).

"No one can fail to remark that this too exclusive dependence on revivals tends to produce a false or unscriptural form of religion. It makes excitement essential to the people, and leads them to think that piety consists in strong exercises of feelings, the nature of which, it is difficult to determine. . . . And all the while, the great means of good, may be entirely neglected. Family training of children, and pastoral instruction of the young, are almost entirely lost sight of. We have long felt and often expressed the conviction that this is one of the most serious evils in the present state of our churches. It is not confined to any one denomination. It is a state of things, which has been gradually induced, and is widely extended. It is therefore one of the great merits of Dr. Bushnell's book, in our estimation, that it directs attention to this very point, and brings prominently forward the defects of our religious views and habits, and points out the appropriate remedy, viz: family religion and Christian nurture." (ps. 520-521).

But while so much of this is cordial and favorable, Dr. Hodge by no means admits the underlying theology. Bushnell's theory seems to Dr. Hodge to rule out the supernatural (though Bushnell claims it does not). "There is here no distinction between God's providential agency and the operations of his grace. He is, according to this doctrine, in no other and in no higher sense the author of regeneration than of a cultivated intellect, or of a majestic tree. The intelligence and skill manifested in fashioning a flower, or forming an eye is not in organic laws, but in those laws as inhabited, to use Dr. B.'s language, by God and his Spirit. . . . Now if conversion, if the regeneration and sanctification of the soul, is only in this sense a supernatural work, then it is as much a natural process, as much the result of organic laws, as any other process of nature whatever. . . . " (p. 526).

Most people today rejoice in the fact that it is the same God whose handiwork is seen in all nature and life and in the heart of man but according to Hodge this identification makes Bushnell "not one inch further advanced than the lowest Rationalists." (p. 527). He will have nothing short of a super supernaturalism. "The whole question is, whether the effect is due to a power that works in nature, or above nature." (p. 530).

The extreme evangelists, according to Bushnell, taught that conversion was sudden. The spirit of God, so to say, struck suddenly and when and how this happened depended on the sovereign will of God alone. This Bushnell called the ictic theory in which God, far removed, acted on the human heart. This characterization of the ictic theory "as God's coming from a state of isolation above, from beyond the fixed stars, from an island where he dwells," (p. 532) sounds to Hodge "profane" and places the theory on a false foundation.

Hodge not only agrees in many points with Bushnell against Tyler but even turns and directly criticizes the latter: "Dr. T. however seems to make less of the promise of God to parents than we do, and to have less reliance on Christian nurture as a means of conversion. We are deeply impressed with the conviction that as to both of these points there is much too low a doctrine now generally prevailing.

And it is because Dr. B. urges the fact of the connexion
between parents and children, with so much power, that
we feel so great an interest in his book. His philosophy of
that fact we hope may soon find its way to the place where
so much philosophy has already gone." (p. 539).

In *The Christian Examiner and Religious Miscellany,* [1]
a Unitarian publication, the reviewer (who signs himself
G. W. B.) says that the book "discusses an important subject; and the argument is conducted in a spirit so rational
and free, so truly Christian, that it must command the admiration of those who may dissent from its conclusions.
Indeed, were its views generally adopted, they would revo-
lutionize the life of the Christian world. . . We propose,
first, to notice the peculiar harmony between the views presented by Dr. Bushnell and those which we have been accus-
tomed to cherish, and, next, to offer a few remarks upon
the main topic of the work itself." (p. 436).

He then goes on presenting the arguments and says that
these are welcome, especially as showing "a growing harmony" in church doctrines and that "they promise to obliterate sectarian division," (p. 439) and adds: "One generation, trained in the spirit of the view which Dr. Bushnell
presents, might banish slavery and war, and many kindred
sins. We rejoice, too, that parental influence is urged by
him so strongly, as a divinely appointed agency for this
great work. No combination of holy influences can com-
pensate for its loss. We mourn, as we consider this, when
we see how the children of numberless homes seem to be

---

[1] Volume XLII.   Fourth Series, Vol. VII.   January, March, May,
1847.   Boston: William Crosby.   November, Art. VIII "Bushnell on
Christian Nurture" (ps. 435-451).

bereaved of their heaven-ordained teachers by the tendencies or the neglect of the time. . . . " (p. 448).

In conclusion, he quotes Bushnell's statement that he "did not draw up this scheme of nurture to meet the uses or gratify the opinions of any sect. It is a first maxim with me, as I think it should be in this age of every one who pretends to think at all, to reach after the most comprehensive form of truth possible; to see how far I may dissolve into unity, in the views I present, the conflicting opinions by which men are divided, giving them back all which they are after, in a form which they can accept together. And the fortune of my little book is, in this view, remarkable, though not a surprise to myself." (ps. 450-451). And the reviewer adds: "A man could not honor himself more than by the avowal of such a principle. It proves him to be worthy of his age. We hail it with joy." (p. 451).

Note that it is this maxim that is welcomed with joy and not necessarily all the teachings of the book. He welcomes Bushnell's criticisms of themselves—the Unitarians—but hopes that "some man amongst ourselves will meet Dr. Bushnell, and all who may sympathize with him, in 'the freedom of conference' he seems to wish, expounding great doctrines from our own point of view, in the same free and catholic spirit. Perhaps no better service could now be done for the religious world." (p. 451).

Some of Bushnell's opponents tried to make a lot out of the "joy" of the Unitarians over his doctrines. But the above quotation shows that this was a twisting, whether deliberate or not, of the actual meaning. Besides, Bushnell pointed out clearly, as indeed this review recognizes, that he differed radically from them on certain fundamental points.

The Christian Review of December, 1847, devoted twenty-two pages to a review of the three publications. [1] As is to be expected, the Baptists sprang to the defence of adult conversion and baptism and to pointing out the errors of Bushnell and of all other pedo-baptists. The reviewer therefore disagrees heartily with Bushnell on these and other points. But he concludes in these words which reveal something of the peculiar power Dr. Bushnell had as a writer:

"Before we take leave of Dr. Bushnell's pamphlets, we wish to add a word more about them and their author. His style is forcible and manly, flexible and eloquent, almost beyond any writer of discourses in New England that we know of. His train of thought is always vigorous and original; he unites singular boldness with great occasional beauty. Never fastidious, and sometimes quite careless; he never tires, but instinctively at the proper moment can rise to great sublimity of thought, and plume a thought with words of exquisite finish, winged words that find their way at once to the heart. . . . Even these discourses on Christian nurture will do good. They will wake up all who read them. . . . (p. 550).

"Still we are bound to express the highest respect and regard for Dr. Bushnell, as a man and as a Christian. His

[1] Vol. XII. Edited by Rev. S. F. Smith, Boston: Rev. William Heath. Utica, N. Y. Bennet, Backus and Hawley, 1847. Article III, ps. 529-551. The title reads as follows: "The Baptist and Pedobaptist theories of Church Membership."

"Discourses on Christian Nurture. By H. Bushnell, D.D. approved by the Publishing Committee of the Massachusetts Sabbath School Society. 1847.

Dr. Tyler's Letter to Dr. Bushnell on Christian Nurture. 1847.

An Argument for "Discourses on Christian Nurture." By Horace Bushnell. Hartford, Edwin Hunt, 6 Asylum Street. 1847."

system has carried him far; for the deeply logical structure
of his mind, and frankness of his character has led him to
avoid all shirking of legitimate consequences; but let it
be here remarked that *this is the mildest and most moderate
theory of infant baptism* ever exhibited; the least offensive
to others, the most simple and consistent with itself. If it
will not stand, nothing will. Dr. Tyler's Letter in reply
to it is but an argument for Baptist principles from beginning to end." (p. 550). This last sentence would not be
soothing to the angry president of The Theological Institute of Connecticut and defender of the true faith!

The New Englander Magazine gives a very favorable
thirty-one page review, [1] which, according to the Index, is
by Dr. Noah Porter. It says in part: "The writer of these
remarks has always believed and preached the doctrine advanced by Dr. Bushnell. He has even preached it in the
same antagonistic form which he has adopted. . . . It is to
be supposed that not a few have held and taught, and sought
to act upon the same opinion. . . . " (p. 123).

He is keen enough to distinguish between Christian
living and theology. "In order that a nurture appropriately
Christian should begin or even take effect," he points out,
"it is *not* necessary that the mind be mature enough to receive Christianity as a system of truth. (p. 129).

" . . . We may safely and reasonably believe, nay, we
may certainly know, that the preparatory influences of the
nursery may blend so gracefully and harmoniously with its
rudimental religious instruction, and both may act so well
together, that as the powers are developed, and the knowl-

---

[1] Vol. VI. January-October, 1848. New Haven: published by A. H.
Maltby, printed by B. L. Hamlen. "Bushnell on Christian Nurture"
January, 1848. ps. 121-147.

edge is enlarged and the habits are matured, there shall
be first a Christian infant, then a Christian child and then
a Christian man." (p. 131).

Yet, though the reviewer claims to have "always believed and preached the doctrine advanced by Dr. Bushnell",
it is quite evident he did not; nor did he grasp its essential
position diametrically opposed to the accepted "conversion"
theory. This the more violent of his opponents sensed if
they did not comprehend.

He gives only a qualified assent to two other positions
of Bushnell: "We should present the two great facts gen-
eralized by Dr. B. as *'organic* laws' and *'individualism'*,
in relative proportions differing considerably from those in
which he employs them." (p. 136).

In the review he also pays his respects to Bushnell's
critics and to the Massachusetts Sabbath School Society:
"To stop the book and give no reason, is to treat the author
and the public with too little consideration, and argues a
liberty of judging and of disposing of a man's good name,
which is not usually entrusted to committees, and which
ought to be exercised by none." (p. 145).

Pointing out certain imperfections in the book, the
critic says, in conclusion: "The doctrine of the book as we
understand it, we think to be true and important." (p. 147).

The review in *The Christian Observatory, a Religious
and Literary Magazine,* [1] merely brings out Tyler's arguments and tries to tie Bushnell up with the Unitarians, because Bushnell said he was glad they approved; but he also
fails to show how Bushnell distinctly contrasts his theories

---

[1] A. W. McClure, editor. Vol. II. June, 1848. "Review. Letters
to Horace Bushnell, D.D. etc. by Bennet Tyler, D.D., 1848". ps. 273-
283.

with theirs. Then the author exclaims: "What, now, think Orthodox men, of Dr. Bushnell?" and advises his friends "not to weary themselves with any farther attempts to maintain that he is a *soundly* Orthodox man." (ps. 279-280). The great sin is to be unorthodox, which means not to accept the position on religious questions held by the Tyler party.

The writer of the review threw down this challenge: "Let the experiment be faithfully tried, whether Dr. Bushnell's book will lie harmoniously by the side of the Bible. We predict that it will be found at variance with the Bible on almost every essential principle entering into the great work of training children for God and heaven." (p. 273). And experience has given an overwhelming verdict against this reviewer's contention.

The Episcopal magazine, *The Church Review and Ecclesiastical Register,* [1] says: "We may say of them (the Discourses), that they are a series of efforts to place the work of promoting and extending religion on a high philosophical ground, to unite and harmonize the various phenomena connected therewith, and to correct the tendencies to fanaticism, which so abundantly prevail in connection with the popular views on the subject. There is a manliness, a comprehensiveness, a richness and fertility of thought in the book, which commands respect and renders the whole attractive." (ps. 228-229).

This is all the stronger statement in view of the fact that in the discriminating review of eighteen pages certain fundamental differences between Bushnell's practice and

---

[1] Vol. I. 1848-1849. New Haven, Conn. Published by Bassett and Bradley. London: George P. Putnam. Article V, in the July, 1848 number, is entitled "Bushnell's Christian Nurture". ps. 228-245.

the Episcopal doctrine are pointed out, as for example, on baptism and "his hostility to the Episcopal Church." (p. 240).

The Methodist Quarterly Review [1] is quite outspoken. The writer says: "Without pledging ourselves to all Dr. Bushnell's views, we yet sympathize far more with him than with the friends in New England he has so terrified. The doctrines of his book, or similar ones, must be proclaimed from our house-tops. No part of the world needs them as do the American churches, with whom baptized children seem to be regarded as little heathens—just as if they had not been baptized at all. . . . We repeat it, from our hearts—on this subject *we need a great awakening*." (p. 156).

From a study of these discriminating and extended reviews in the leading religious magazines of several denominations it is evident that Bushnell's writings had made a profound impression; that, while disagreeing on certain points, the remarkable thing is that in a day when theological lines were strictly drawn there is such agreement with his main thesis; and that his views, while recognized as revolutionary, were welcomed, except by Tyler and his party, as a wholesome emphasis in religious thought and practice.

----

[1] January, 1849.

CHAPTER IV

BUSHNELL AND TYLER

TYLER, as has been shown, had a number of excuses for springing to the defence of the faith of the past. After his first letter which brought him the satisfaction of having the book withdrawn by the Massachusetts Sabbath School Society he published seven others. Bushnell's reply is in his *Argument*, so there is no duel of letters. In Tyler's there is a great deal of repetition, as he insists on several doctrines and judges everything in their light. He also seeks to use, with all his skill, techniques too often found employed by politicians and ecclesiastics. Perhaps Tyler saw more clearly than some that if Bushnell were right, fundamental doctrines of the orthodox theologians would have to be abandoned.

Bushnell's central theory is *That the child is to grow up a Christian* [1] (p. 6). But he guards this statement: "I do not affirm that every child may, in fact and without exception, be so trained that he certainly will grow up a Christian." (p. 7). He shows that "this doctrine is not a novelty" but is as old as Christianity and that there is "no absurdity in supposing that children are to grow up in Christ" but "a very clear, moral incongruity in setting up

---

[1] *Discourses on Christian Nurture.* Boston, Massachusetts Sabbath School Society, 1847. In later editions this is expanded into his famous dictum *That the child is to grow up a Christian, and never know himself as being otherwise.*

49

a contrary supposition, to be the aim of a system of Christian education." (p. 12). And he says further, "There are many who assume the radical goodness of human nature, and the work of Christian education is, in their view, only to educate, or educe the good that is in us. Let no one be disturbed by the suspicion of a coincidence between what I have here said and such a theory." (p. 21).

To this doctrine that a child may grow up a Christian, Tyler replies with what he believes to be one of his crushing syllogisms: "That the child should grow up a Christian, it is necessary that he should become a Christian. And how is he to become a Christian?"[1] And then he lays down one of his bedrock "Facts": "It is a fundamental principle of the Christian scheme", he alleges, "that every child born into the world, is by nature totally depraved, and must be born again in order to become a child of God, and an heir of heaven." (p. 3). Thus he meets argument and common sense by increased dogmatism. He was right to this extent, that either position had to be given up and there is now little dispute as to which it is.

But he goes one step further: "I readily grant that God can, if he sees fit, renew, by his Spirit, the heart of a child as soon as he is born. . . . But the question at issue, relates not to what God is able to do. He is doubtless able to renew the heart of every child, born either of religious or irreligious parents; but this does not prove that he will do it." (p. 4).

"No Christian instruction, or Christian discipline, could have any instrumentality in the child's conversion.

---

[1] Tyler, Bennet. *Letter to the Rev. Horace Bushnell, D.D.* Read at the annual meeting of the North Association of Hartford County. East Windsor Hill, June 7, 1847. p. 3.

... Such instances may occur, in answer to the prayers of God's people, but they are to be attributed to the sovereign act of God, independently of all human instrumentality. ... Every child comes into the world depraved, and until renewed by the Holy Ghost, is spiritually dead. ... (p. 4). If a child, born of human parents, were educated by angels, amid the glories of heaven, he would grow up a sinner, unless renewed by the power of the Holy Ghost. ... In this, he acts as a holy sovereign, as he does in all his dispensations. ... " (p. 6). Therefore if children or others are not "converted" it is because God has not, in his supreme wisdom, seen fit to perform "the sovereign act." So avers Tyler.

Bushnell said that parents were not always safe judges as to children's religious nature: "You may be unreasonable in your expectations of your children. Possibly, there may be seeds of holy principle in them, which you do not discover. ... It is conceivable that regenerate character may exist, long before it is fully and formally developed." [1] This provoked Tyler to wrath. "No parent has a right to assume," he thunders, "that some 'seeds of holy principle' have been implanted in the heart of his child, till he sees some evidence of the fact. He is taught in the scriptures, that his child is, by nature, a child of wrath, even as others—that he is born depraved, with a nature prone to evil, and that he will continue so, till renewed by the Holy Spirit." (p. 8).

In his argument on organic connection Bushnell had expressed a great truth now amply substantiated. "A pure, separate, individual man, living *wholly* within, and from himself, is a mere fiction. No such person ever existed, or

---

[1] *Discourses on Christian Nurture.* p. 8.

ever can." [1] This he sees must modify the New England theology and religious education based on a misleading individualism.

He continues, "I need not say that this view of an organic connection of character subsisting between parent and child, lays a basis for notions of Christian education, far different from those which now prevail, under the cover of a merely fictitious and mischievous individualism." (p. 32).

Tyler is filled with fear (how unnecessary it was!) lest parents, and children also, would presume on inherited goodness to their own destruction. This is one of the "dangerous tendencies" in the little book. "There are other parts of your discourses" he wrote "which are fraught with the same dangerous tendency; particularly what you say of an *organic connection* subsisting between parents and their children, and the subject of Infant Baptism. . . . (p. 9). Other things which you have said, seem to imply that piety, in your view, is hereditary in the same sense that depravity is." (p. 10). If this is so, he says, goodness might also be inherited. That goodness should in any way be inherited was to him unthinkable while making basic the doctrine that total depravity was inescapably hereditary.

Bushnell told the story of a young man who became a Christian without having any deep struggle. [2] This Tyler "cannot but regard as containing error of a very dangerous tendency." He waxes hot and scornful. "And this is considered genuine conversion. And the person thus con-

---

[1] Op. cit. p. 32.

[2] *Discourses on Christian Nurture.* p. 17.

verted is said to be 'henceforth to the end of a long and
useful life, a Christian man,' and 'one of the most beautiful, healthful, and dignified examples of Chrisian piety.'

"Now all this is a fancy sketch. It is not drawn from
real life. Such a conversion I cannot believe, ever did, or
ever will result in a life of genuine piety. . . . " (ps. 12-13).

Bushnell had said that in spite of certain weaknesses
in their church work "the German people are every day
spoken of as a people religious by nature."[1] This also
arouses Tyler's ire. He has no love for "foreigners", especially for Germans, as has already appeared. In irrita-
tion he exclaims "And suppose they are religious by nature.
They are not the only people of whom this may be affirmed
with truth. . . . Men may be *religious* by nature. But they
are not *Christians* by nature." (ps. 15-16).

Bushnell told of a little book he thought misleading.[2]
It described "a lovely boy who was called every day, to resolve that he would do no wrong that day, a task which he
undertook most cheerfully, at first, and even with a show
of delight. But, before the sun went down, he was sure
to fall into some ill-temper or be overtaken by some infirmity. Whereupon, the conclusion was immediately
sprung upon him that he wanted a new heart. We are even
amazed that any teacher of ordinary intelligence should
not once have imagined how she herself, or how the holiest
Christian living would fare under such kind of regimen?
And the practical cruelty of the experiment is yet more to
be deplored, than its want of consideration. Had the problem been how to discourage most effectually every ingenuous

---

[1] Ibid. p. 25.

[2] Ibid. ps. 54-55.

struggle of childhood, no readier or surer method could have been devised."

But Tyler has the directly opposite view, and the clash reveals a difference in natures. Tyler says, "I know not that I ever saw the book of which you speak. But your account of it, has led me to think it is probably a very good and useful book. The object I cannot but regard as very important, viz. 'to teach a child that he wants a new heart.' . . . The manner of teaching this lesson, strikes me as particularly happy. . . . If the child is not to be taught that he needs a new heart, for what would you teach him to pray?" (p. 17).

Bushnell had said that if, as the orthodox maintained, the only way to become a Christian is through a deep sense of sin and a conversion experience and if one can do nothing good until by the will of God that takes place, why should he try to be good? "He must have a new heart *before* he can be good." [1] To have a new heart he must have conviction of sin. In other words "Children are to grow up in sin. . . . " [2] Tyler accepts the premises, but rejects the conclusion with scorn. He says, "I must repel the insinuation as unjust and slanderous." (p. 18). But he cannot escape the dilemma with all his casuistry.

He concludes this first attack (which the Association asked to have printed and which so scared the Massachusetts Sabbath School Society) with this much commendation: "I should do you injustice not to say, that there are some things in your discourse, of which I highly approve. So far as it is your aim to stimulate parents to more de-

---

[1] Op. cit. p. 55.
[2] Ibid. p. 59.

voted and self-denying labor in the education of their children, the object is certainly commendable. What you say with a design to impress on their minds the importance of making 'the first article of family discipline, a constant and careful discipline of themselves,' is particularly excellent. This cannot be too strenuously urged. It is a point in which all parents more or less fail." (p. 21).

Bushnell's answer appeared in the *Argument*. As already seen in his reply to Bishop Brownell (ps. 7-8), he was wonderfully equipped for controversy and, to those who enjoy the joined battle, passages in the *Argument* are stimulating reading. His method is so different from Tyler's that the two are a striking contrast. Tyler stands for the letter and is not overscrupulous as to how he gains his point; Bushnell stands for the spirit and the larger interpretation and life.

Here is one sample of his scathing reply provoked by the precipitate surrender of the Committee and by Tyler's galling attack: "No word of complaint against my tract had you heard, till you heard it from Connecticut. . . . That you, a numerous and respectable committee, after having come to a serious and careful decision on my *Discourses,* a decision matured by six months of deliberation, should have turned pale and recanted, at the first note of disapprobation from Connecticut, is, to say the least, more than we could have expected." [1]

---

[1] *An Argument for "Discourses on Christian Nurture"*. Addressed to the Publishing Committee of the Massachusetts Sabbath School Society. Hartford, Edwin Hunt, 1847. This first appeared as a pamphlet and was later republished in his *Views of Christian Nurture, and of Subjects Adjacent Thereto*. Page references to the argument will be given to both, thus: *Argument* ps. 27-28; *Views* p. 87. Other quotations from Bushnell on Christian Nurture previously from the *Discourses* are now taken from the *Views*.

Then he pays his respects to Tyler and the Theological
Institute of Connecticut of which he was president: [1] "We
have a little institution sworn, every six months to suffer
no progress, also to maintain the new light doctrine as
equivalent to all antiquity, and probably fulfilling its oaths
with religious fidelity—therefore certain, as we suppose
you will see, to condemn others with as little reason as it
is permitted to exercise for itself. It has three professors
and twelve or fifteen students, and calls off one or two
ministers from their charge, a considerable part of the time,
to gather up the requisite funds." (p. 28; 87-88).

In the first part of the *Argument* Bushnell shows that
the position he advocates is not new but is as old as the
Christian church. It is the narrow individualism of Edwards and the "New Light" movement that was an inno-
vation and out of harmony with the early church doctrines
and practice. In this Hodge supports Bushnell, and while
it is generally acknowledged today, it would be well for
many to refresh their minds on the matter. Bushnell
quotes many authorities including New Testament writers,
ancient inscriptions, and Christian writers giving exact
source references with meticulous care. Only a few
samples will be given.

" 'In such a life, the new birth was not to constitute a
new crisis beginning at some definable moment, but it was
to begin imperceptibly, and so proceed through the whole
life.' *Neander's Church History, Torrey's Translation*, p.
311, '12" (p. 7; 55). " 'Gregory Nazianzen peculiarly commends his mother, that not only she herself was consecrated
to God and brought up under a pious education, *but that*

---

[1] He never replied to Tyler's persistent persecution again, though
this was misunderstood, nor to any of his opponents in harsh language.

she conveyed it down, as a necessary inheritance, to her children.' . . . *Primitive Christianity,* p. 173, '4' " (p. 7; 55-56). Baxter he quotes as saying that "godly education" by parents is "God's first and ordinary appointed means for the begetting of actual faith" in children, "and public preaching is appointed for the conversion of those only that missed the blessing of the first appointed means. . . . *Christian Directory, vol. II. cap. 6, #4, folio, p. 516."* (p. 10; 60). Even Edwards was disappointed in revivalism, for he said: "I cannot say that the greater part of supposed converts give reason, by their conversation, to suppose that they continue converts. The proportion may perhaps be more truly represented by the proportion of blossoms on a tree, which abide and come to mature fruit, to the whole number of blossoms in the spring.' *Life,* 460." (p. 15; 67).

He points out that Tyler's opposition is based on "a certain theory of depravity and regeneration that was de-bated, to the complete satisfaction of the public, some fifteen years ago, and, as I believe, forever exploded." (p. 29; 89). This is a polite way of showing that Tyler was considerably behind the times. Then he adds: "According to this theory the human race hate God instinctively, and must hate him the more, the more clearly his character is seen, until after a certain divine stroke or *ictus* reverses the instinct, when love results as hatred did before." (p. 29; 89).

Bushnell himself had the courage to give up positions which did not satisfy his mind and heart. In his day it was held (as it is in some communions today) that infant baptism changed the nature of the child. This perplexed him, but thinking it over, the light came. Though inter-preting infant baptism in a new way, he yet holds to it as a beautiful and significant rite and even hopes that the

Baptists will so come to regard it. Bushnell's own words
are as follows: "After two or three years of reflection, I
came upon the discovery that all my views of Christian
nurture were radically defective and even false. And now
what before was dark or even absurd, immediately became
luminous and dignified—a rite the most beautiful and appropriate of all the ordinances of God. And when our
Baptist brethren can take up this view of Christian nurture,
I think they will discover that, while we have been in as
great error as they—perhaps even greater because of our
inconsistency—God has yet saved us a rite, which may be
as true a comfort and as rich a blessing to themselves as
to us." (p. 24; 82).

The theory of "organic unity" was misunderstood
either wilfully or otherwise. He clarifies his position in the
following statement, which is on the whole quite in keeping
with modern thought: "I set up the term *'organic'* to contrast in idea with *'individual'*, both as theologic or meta-
physical terms, not as physical. . . . I take my stand at the
birth point of the will (not of the body), and there I say
that the Christian child ought to emerge into *individuality*,
not as ripened into sin and set off in it, but as one that is
regenerated, quickened unto spiritual life. . . . At some
time, sooner or later, but only by a gradual transition, he
comes into his own will, which, theologically speaking, is
the time of his birth as a moral subject of God's government; and if he takes up life as a corrupted subject, so he
may and ought also to take it up as a renewed subject—
that is to *grow up as a Christian*." (ps. 32; 94-95).

It is against this individualism, the ictic idea of God's
method of action, and "the unit or atom theory of religion"

that he develops his organic idea of society. Along with this in the ictic theory is included his intense opposition to the idea of the "expectation of Christian nurture" being on "the other side of the fixed stars" so that "if any good comes to the child, it must come straight down from the island occupied by Jehovah, to the child as an individual." (p. 36; 100). He stands for the supernatural operating in and through nature and human life. He was perfectly aware of the far reaching character of his theory (as was Tyler also), and frankly points out that he is "dissolving . . . all the doctrines of depravity held by all the sects." (ps. 32-33; 95).

He is surprised that some critics should accuse him of naturalism. "But I meant to interpose all the safeguards necessary to save myself from proper naturalism, and I supposed that I had done it. I really think so now. The very first sentence of my tract is a declaration of supernaturalism. I find too that, in as many as thirteen distinct passages, I have used language that has no proper signification at all, unless it carries the idea, either of a supernatural redemption, or of a want that requires it." (p. 36; 100). To understand this fully, it would be necessary to go into his book on *Nature and the Supernatural*. The "orthodox" view made a hard and fast line between nature and the supernatural which amounted practically to dualism. But Bushnell anticipated in a remarkable way the whole scientific movement which makes it easy to see God in the laws and processes of nature.

He pleads that the church may throw all its strength into the religious nurture of children, so that they may grow up Christians rather than sin-sick souls for future conversion. In other words, he believes "that there is a

dispensation of the Spirit for all ages; one appropriate to
the adult, and one appropriate to the rudimental and un-
reflective age previous to moral action." (p. 38; 103).

Bushnell perceives that many errors are made because
people do not take pains actually to know children and also
in thinking that nothing is learned except through "instruction". These causes are equally fruitful in producing
errors today. He says: "Many persons seem never to
have brought their minds down close enough to an infant
child to understand that any thing of consequence is going
on with it, until after it has come to language and become
a subject of *instruction*. As if a child were to learn a
language before it is capable of learning any thing!" Then
he adds this, which anticipates wonderfully the present day
conviction: "I strongly suspect that more is done, in the
age previous to language, to affect the character of children,
whether by parents, or, when they are waiting in indolent
security, by nurses and attendants, than in all the instruction and discipline of their minority afterwards." (ps. 39;
105-106).

This being so, he makes an ardent plea for parents
not only to teach religion, but to be Christian. "I wish to
produce an impression that God has not held us responsible
for the effect only of what we do, or teach, or for acts of
control and government; but quite as much, for the effect
of *our being what we are;* that there is a plastic age in the
house, receiving its type, not from our words but from our
spirit, one whose character is shaping in the molds of our
own." (p. 40; 106-107). These two paragraphs express
fundamental convictions today.

By emphasis on conversion instead of nurture, the
gradual development of habits and good character is

neglected, Bushnell asserted. The test for church membership is a type of emotional experience rather than Christian living. "We make nothing of habit, nothing of a proposed aim of life connected with Christian duties, but we demand a kind of religious experience that stands in marked contrast with the previous time, particularly in regard to feelings of complacency towards God. . . . And this new rhapsody, this strange kindling of enthusiasm, he is sure must be Christian love,—now his sins are forgiven, and his peace with God is sealed! On precisely this kind of evidence generally, converts are accepted as such at the door of the church, and admitted to the interior rites of discipleship. In fact, no evidence of Christian character is considered so decisive, as that which is found in a change of emotions." (ps. 43-44; 111-113).

Then with words that have the ring of a "Thus saith the Lord" of an Old Testament prophet, he spoke words that were perhaps truer than he knew: "Brethren, whether you will believe it or not, a new day has come. If we will, we can make it a better day, but it demands a furniture of thought and feeling, such as we must stretch ourselves in a degree to realize." (p. 48; 121).

Tyler, as already pointed out, kept up a running fire of letters against Bushnell. In the following pages in this chapter all the references are to this series of seven letters published as pamphlets. [1] To these, as already stated, Bushnell, with great restraint, made no reply.

Tyler's seven letters reiterate the cardinal points of orthodoxy and the effect must have steeled all like-thinking

---

[1] For particulars see the bibliography. References here will be written briefly as Letter I, Letter II, and so on.

readers into a solid mindset against the object of his attack, though his hounding and his type of argument alienated many thoughtful people.

"It seems to me," he says, "you virtually deny the doctrines of total depravity, and of regeneration by the special agency of the Holy Spirit." (Letter IV, p. 39). He, of course, thus attacks the central thesis "that the child is to grow up a Christian". "By the phrase 'To open on the world, as one that is spiritually renewed,' I understand you to mean, to be a Christian from the commencement of moral agency. . . . You do not undertake to decide when moral agency and individual accountability commence; but your theory, if I understand it, is, that the child, properly trained, will at that point, 'open on the world' a Christian. You thus make the parent responsible for the character of his child." (Letter II, p. 12). Now the last sentence is an example of Tyler's unfair tactics. It could scarcely be due to obtuseness, unless he was blinded by prejudice and anger. Bushnell did strive to lead parents to feel their responsibility as teachers and fellow workers with God. His very sentence is a "nurture which is of the Lord, deriving a quality and a power from Him, and communicating the same." [1]

Dr. Tyler presents a good example of the syllogistic "reasoning" of the time: "You say, 1. 'There is no absurdity in supposing that children are to grow up in Christ.' Be it so. What then? Have we reason to expect a thing will certainly take place, because there is no absurdity in supposing that it may take place? . . . Your argument reduced to a syllogism, stands thus.

---

[1] *Discourses on Christian Nurture.* p. 1.

"There is reason to believe that a thing will take place, if there is no absurdity in supposing that it may take place.

"But there is no absurdity in supposing that the children of pious parents who are faithfully trained, may grow up in Christ.

"Therefore—there is reason to believe that such children will grow up in Christ.

"You say, 2. 'It is to be expected that Christian education will radically differ from that which is not Christian'. Very true. . . . But are we hence to conclude, that all who hear the true gospel, will be immediately converted?

"You say, 3. 'It is a fact that all Christian parents would like to see their children grow up in piety'. . . . That God is able to renew the heart of an infant, is not disputed. But the question is, whether, if parents are faithful, he will, as a general thing, renew thus early, the hearts of their children." (Letter II, ps. 13-14).

Tyler and his type are very insistent that the unregenerate, the totally depraved, can do nothing for himself. It depends not on *"the will of man—but of God.* Such power does not belong to man. It is God's work to renew the heart." (Letter II, p. 14). And, of course, God may not will so to do! The case is put unmistakably that "all children being born depraved, are by nature children of wrath, and will continue to be such, till God shall renew their hearts—and that God will have mercy not only *on whom,* but *when* he will have mercy." (Letter VII, p. 73). "The distinction between Esau and Jacob was made, not on account of a difference in their Christian nurture, but 'that the purpose of God according to election might stand.'" (Letter II, p. 25). It is interesting to note that these two Old Testament worthies had *Christian* nurture!

"You say," Tyler writes, " 'according to all that God has taught us, concerning his own dispositions, he desires on his part, that children should grow up in piety as earnestly as the parent can desire it; nay, as much more earnestly, as he hates sin more intensely, and desires good with less mixture, or qualification.'

"Do you mean by this statement that God so desires the holiness of all children, that he will sanctify them in infancy? . . . . May there be no 'collateral reasons in his plan,' which may induce him to delay the bestowment of his renewing grace? God is wont to try the faith of his people." Then he waxes sarcastic: "It is undoubtedly true, that in the Millennium children will be converted early. But it remains to be proved, that they will *then* be pious from the commencement of their moral existence. . . . 'A time is foretold,' when the man of sin shall be destroyed, when Mohammedan delusion, pagan idolatry, and Jewish infidelity shall come to an end." (Letter II, ps. 17-20). Tyler's antipathy to other races and religions comes out spontaneously.

Then he is dreadfully afraid of spiritual pride or presumption. Tyler can give no quarter to the thought that any child can possibly have any holy principle in him. "My objection to what you had affirmed was, that it encouraged parents to presume that their children were pious, when they not only gave no evidence of the fact, but when they seemed 'intractable to religious influences,' and 'displayed an apparent aversion to the very subject of religion itself.' . . . One of the ways in which you attempt to account for it, and that against which my objection is made, is, that notwithstanding these outward appearances, their 'children may have seeds of holy principle in them' which are not yet discovered. . . . It is to this that I object." (Letter I, ps. 8-9).

But even if all are totally depraved, Bushnell advanced the obvious argument that the best time to develop the new life is in the growing days of childhood, but Tyler will have none of it.

"You say, 4. 'Assuming the corruption of human nature, when should we think it wisest to undertake, or to expect a remedy? When evil is young and pliant to good, or when it is confirmed by years of sinful habit?' 'When should *we* think it wisest?' " he almost screams, *"We!* Are *we* competent to decide what it is wisest for God to do? . . . And why have most of those who have hitherto been made the trophies of redeeming grace, lived some years, at least, in impenitence and unbelief? . . . Every child is by nature spiritually dead; and no power short of that which can raise the dead, is adequate to impart spiritual life. 'You hath he quickened, who were dead in trespasses and sins.'

"It is true, that the minds of children are very susceptible of religious impressions. . . . But they never change the moral disposition. This can be done only by the special agency of the Holy Spirit. . . . No one doubts that God can renew the heart of a child. But the question is, whether we are warranted to suppose he will, as a general thing, renew the hearts of children in infancy, if their parents are faithful.

"You say, 5. 'It is implied in all of our religious philosophy, that if a child ever does any thing in a right spirit, ever loves any thing because it is good and right, it involves the dawn of a new life. . . .'

"I answer—Not at all incredible, if God shall see fit to renew the heart of the child. But does this prove that the child of every Christian parent who is faithful, will 'open on the world as one that is spiritually renewed?' Far from it." (Letter II, ps. 14-15).

If any one is to grow up good, it is a miracle and involves the miraculous, special agency of God. That it should be according to God's laws is spurned with something approaching venom. "According to these representations how is the Christian character formed in the children of believers? Not by any special divine agency, but by the regular operation of the physical laws of our being. . . . Your idea, if I understand you, is, that none of the laws of nature operate independently of God—that second causes are not complete causes in themselves, but are dependent on an all-pervading divine influence. Such an influence I understand you to admit in the formation of the Christian character." (Letter IV, p. 41).

The "ictic theory" is the only one for "safe" leaders: "This aid, however, you suppose to be always at his command. . . . The doctrine of special grace, therefore, has no place in your system. . . . This is the 'ictic theory' which you have made the theme of ridicule. No sir, you must find some other way of accounting for the fact in question, or give up your system." (Letter IV, ps. 41-42). There is thus no foundation for believing that one can always count on the aid of God. If the child grows up a Christian, Bushnell holds it is "with the aid of divine influence," which may always be counted on. But, objects Tyler, this is a false assumption.

Bushnell had said that many (including Baxter) had grown up Christians. Tyler denies this fact so well substantiated in the New Testament and through the history of the church and gladly admitted today. "You say, ' . . .

Children have been so trained as never to remember the time when they began to be religious.' Be it so. How many of this description can be found? Read over the biographies of good men—and of those especially whose parents were distinguished examples of parental fidelity. And how many will you find, who could not remember the time when they began to be religious? Go through the churches of New England (and in what other churches on the globe will you find more genuine piety?), and how large a proportion of the members will tell you, they cannot remember the time when they were dead in trespasses and sins? Probably not one in fifty." (Letter II, ps. 15-16).

It will be noticed that Tyler makes many dogmatic assertions without any attempt to prove them, a habit of many theologians of his day.

As already appears, the opponents lost no opportunity of trying to identify Bushnell with some opprobrious ism and to label him with its tag, so transferring to him all the prejudice and animosity felt against it. This is an old device still greatly used in debate and propaganda. "Permit me also to ask, how it has happened, that the Unitarians, who have no sympathy with the views of Hopkins, West and Dwight, are highly pleased with your discourses? . . . (Letter III, p. 26). The doctrine of instantaneous regeneration by the special agency of the Holy Spirit, I understand you utterly discard. The divine influence which you admit in the formation of the Christian character, amounts to no more than what the Unitarians generally admit; and this accounts for the fact that the Unitarians are so well pleased with your book." (Letter IV, p. 42).

"Now you are not ignorant of the fact, that Unitarians deny the doctrine of man's entire depravity, and the doctrine of regeneration by the special agency of the Holy Spirit. . . . " (Letter IV, p. 43).

Having made Bushnell a Unitarian, he applies the body blow of the dilemma. He must admit he is a Unitarian or that he tried to deceive. It is the old device "Is it lawful to give tribute to Caesar, or not?"[1] "You either intended to deceive the Unitarians, and are very happy to find that you have done it, or you and they do substantially agree on the points in question—points not of mere speculation, but of great practical importance."

Now comes the knockout! "And would you have them admitted to Christian fellowship? Would you have orthodox ministers exchange pulpits with the Unitarians, and orthodox churches admit Unitarians to their communion?" No one can justly accuse Tyler of being internationally minded or of making for denominational rapprochement. Such an accusation he would consider a slander! He continues sarcastically: "Have the Unitarians and the orthodox of Massachusetts been approximating towards each other in their theological views, during the last thirty years? Who among the orthodox will be willing to allow this to be true in relation to themselves? Who among them will not spurn the imputation as a slander? And have the Unitarians become more evangelical in their views? There is a class of Unitarians, I am aware, who have assumed the appearance of greater seriousness than has heretofore been manifested by the sect; and there is another class, represented by Theodore Parker, who have outstripped their brethren in infidelity and blasphemy; but point me to any Unitarians in New England, who believe the whole Bible to be given by divine inspiration, or who

---

[1] Mk. 12:14, Lk. 20:22.

believe the doctrines of the Trinity, of total depravity, of vicarious atonement, of justification by faith, of regeneration by the special agency of the Holy Spirit, or of the eternal punishment of the wicked. Take away these doctrines, and what of Christianity have we left? . . . (Letter IV, ps. 43-44). The motto of Theodore Parker is progress; and so rapid has been his progress, that although he still claims to be a Christian preacher, he can revile the scriptures equal to any infidel, Thomas Paine himself not excepted." (Letter IV, p. 45).

It is difficult to believe that Tyler should deliberately misrepresent. But in his *Argument* Bushnell devotes several pages [1] to the Unitarians in which he points out with his usual frankness his distinct and strong opposition to them on certain points, but he is as keen to bring about a better mutual understanding with them and with other denominations as Tyler is to prevent any such weakening of divisions.

He also attempts to ally the pastors with himself. Referring to a passage in which Bushnell refers slightingly to the East Windsor Hill seminary, he says "It is perfectly obvious that the whole passage was intended to hold up to contempt the Pastoral Union of Connecticut, and those friends and patrons of the seminary who are wont to assemble at the time of its anniversaries. But let me tell you that this body of men, is not a contemptible clan, which can be put down with a sneer." (Letter VII, p. 79).

He appeals also to New England provincialism and "hundred percent Americanism" and shows no symptoms of the disease of internationalism. "Will you now permit me to ask, where will you find a better type of religion than that which has prevailed in New England for the last hun-

---

[1] *Argument*, ps. 26-27; 85-87.

dred years? That there is, and ever has been, much to
deplore in our churches, is undoubtedly true. But where
on the globe, will you find a cluster of churches in which
there has been more vital godliness than in the Congregational churches of New England? . . . Will you find it in
the church of England, or in the church of Scotland, or
among the dissenters in England, or among the Lutheran,
or German Reformed Churches, in this country or in Europe? Or will you find it among the Rationalists of Germany, or the Unitarians at home?" (Letter VI, ps. 68-69).

A great deal has been made of Bushnell's reference to
Germany as if he were setting it up as an example of saint-
liness. All he said was that their religious life was " 'remarkable' only as contrasted with the 'looseness' and the
'pernicious error' prevalent in their 'pulpits.' " His point
was that if, in spite of this, they were still religious, it was
because "they are under a form of treatment that expects
them to be religious." [1] From this distance Bushnell seems
justified in considering that his opponents are, on this point,
guilty of misrepresentation.

Tyler had written a book on revivals and is sensitive
to any attack on them. "Read the narratives of revivals
in the Old Connecticut Evangelical Magazine, which occurred fifty years ago. You will there learn what the
preaching was in those days, and what were its effects. In
those revivals, the following doctrines were dwelt upon,
and exhibited with great plainness—The sinner's entire depravity—his obligation to be holy—his inexcusableness for
continuing a moment in impenitence and unbelief—the
utter worthlessness of all his unregenerate doings—his un-
willingness to come to Christ for salvation, and his conse-

---

[1] *Argument*, p. 31; 93.

quent dependence on the sovereign mercy of God—and God's perfect right to do with him as should seem good in his sight. (Letter VI, p. 67).

"My Dear Sir, the only 'passions kindled' in the hearts of unrenewed men by a contemplation of 'the beauty and glory of God' as he is revealed in the scriptures, are the passions of hatred and disgust. It is a contradiction in terms to say that the true character of God may appear beautiful and glorious to a person whose heart is enmity against him." (Letter VI, p. 68)

One of Bushnell's big contributions was his pointing out that the Christian religion had self-propagating power. His words are vital now, and need to be heeded by the church. He is opposed to the policy of conquest at home and in mission work. It is safe to say that the church as a whole agrees with him on this point and is trying to act accordingly. He said: "Our very theory of religion is, that men are to grow up in evil, and be dragged into the church of God by conquest. The world is to lie in halves, and the kingdom of God is to stretch itself side by side with the kingdom of darkness, making sallies into it, and taking captive those who are sufficiently hardened and bronzed in guiltiness to be converted." [1] Edwards and other New England divines he speaks of as "Hanging every thing thus on miracle, or a pure *ictus Dei,* separate from all instrumental connexions of truth, feeling, dependence, motive and choice, there was manifestly nothing left but to wait for the concussion." [2] "Religion is thus a kind of transcendental matter, which belongs on the outside of life, and has no part in the laws by which life is organized—a mir-

---

[1] *Views of Christian Nurture*, ps. 25-26.

[2] *Argument*, p. 14; 66.

aculous epidemic, a fire ball shot from the moon, something
holy because it is from God. . . . " [1] He pointed out that
"Revivals, themselves, have sunk into a formality; and
what is even more singular, conversions also." [2]—to which
Tyler answered: "Genuine revivals, and *genuine* conversions cannot sink into a formality. What you affirm, therefore, is equivalent to the assertion, that genuine revivals,
and genuine conversions have ceased to exist. And is it
so? . . . That there have been during the last twenty years,
not a few spurious revivals, and great numbers of spurious
conversions, there is reason to believe. . . . I fear that in
New England even there is not so much plain, solemn,
searching preaching, as there was in the days of our
fathers." (Letter VII, p. 78). And then he speaks again
to the galleries: "If deep spiritual piety ever existed in any
churches on the globe, it has existed in the churches of New
England; and as the result too, of pure and powerful revivals of religion." (Letter VII, p. 78).

Bushnell said, further: "If you will attend the General
Association of Connecticut, or of Massachusetts, and listen
to the reports on the state of religion, you will discover, although it may not be uniformly said, that a year which has
brought no revivals of religion is considered to be of course
a barren year." [3] And Tyler's reply is: "Do you mean to
intimate that there is no reason for these representations?"
(Letter V, p. 51).

Again, Bushnell wrote: "No nation can long thrive
by a spirit of conquest; no more can a church. There must

---

[1] Ibid, p. 16; 69.

[2] *Views of Christian Nurture, and of Subjects Adjacent Thereto*,
p. 241.

[3] *Argument*, p. 41; 109.

be an internal growth, that is made by holy industry, in the common walks of life and duty." [1] Tyler rejoins: "You have much to say about depending on 'growth' for the up-building of the church, and not on 'conquest'. And 'revivals of religion so called,' you say, 'are our scenes of conquest.' . . . Permit me to express the opinion that the kingdom of Christ never has made, and never will make any progress in this world, except by conquest. This is a world of rebels. It is so represented in the Scriptures. 'I have nourished and brought up children, and they have rebelled against me.' 'The carnal mind is enmity against God.' Every man, by nature, is arrayed in hostility against his Maker. . . . All the subjects of Christ's kingdom on earth, have been gained by conquest. Hence Christ is exhibited in the Scriptures as a mighty conqueror. . . . Yes, it is by conquest that this world is to be converted to Christ. (Letter V, p. 53). But you think the church ought to increase by 'growth', and not by *'conquest'*. Growth! What is there to grow? Religion cannot grow, before it begins to exist; and there is not a heart in which it has an existence, till that heart has been gained by conquest. When God by his invincible grace has changed the heart of a sinner, we may then expect he will grow in grace." (Letter V, p. 54).

He goes on to say "The truth is, such is the desperate wickedness of the human heart, that it will yield to no means which can be employed. . . . Nothing but the Omnipotent energy of the Holy Spirit can do it. 'Not by might nor by power, but by my Spirit, saith the Lord.' " (Letter V, p. 59). His appeal to the apostles in the same letter (ps. 58-59) is an anti-climax, for their experience substantiates

---

[1] *Views*, ps. 44-45.

Bushnell's claim. They exhibit gradual growth not only during the lifetime of Jesus, but also afterwards.

Continuing, Tyler says: "But what is the remedy which you propose for this bad 'type of religion,' of which you complain? If I understand you, it is, that we should cease to depend on 'conquest' for the continuance and increase of the church, and begin to depend on a natural and internal growth,—that we should think less of revivals of religion, and more of Christian education." (Letter VI, p. 69). One of the most remarkable tendencies of recent times both as to the home church and foreign missions is the turning from methods of conquest to developing the indigenous life of the people especially by the propagating power of friendship, love, and service through "the loveliness of the good life," in fellowship with God.

Another point at issue was Bushnell's theory of organic connection in the family. So much controversy stormed around this that it must be quoted. ". . . . If we narrowly examine the relation of parent and child, we shall not fail to discover something like a law of organic connection, as regards character, subsisting between them. Such a connection as makes it easy to believe, and natural to expect that the faith of one will be propagated in the other. Perhaps I should rather say, such a connection as induces the conviction that the character of one is actually included in that of the other, as a seed is formed in the capsule; and being there matured, by a nutriment derived from the stem, is gradually separated from it. It is a singular fact, that many believe substantially the same thing, in regard to evil character, but have no thought of any such possibility in regard to good." [1]

_____

[1] *Views*, p. 18.

Notice how careful the statement is—"something like a law of organic connection" so that "the faith of one" may be expected to "be propagated in the other."

Tyler examines the Old Testament covenant with Abraham, and says that "By the seed of Abraham, therefore, with whom God said he would establish his covenant to be a God unto them, were meant all who from that time to the end of the world, would become believers in Christ." (Letter III, p. 34). This view, however impossible to liberals now, was commonly believed. He concludes, in rebuttal of Bushnell's position, that "There is no promise in this covenant, that if parents are faithful their children will *all* be pious; much less, that they will, as a general thing, be pious as soon as they are moral agents." (Letter III, 6. 38).

Now, Bushnell had never claimed that "*all* would be pious." He said specifically "I do not affirm that every child may, in fact and without exception, be so trained that he certainly will grow up a Christian," but that "the aim, effort and expectation should be" that the child would grow up a Christian. This seems today not to be an exaggerated statement.

But Tyler reiterates: "Every child, whatever be the character of his parents, is born totally depraved, and spiritually dead, and will continue so, till spiritual life be imparted from on high." (Letter III, p. 38).

In order that the church might visualize the fact that children are members, Bushnell wishes there might be some form of partial membership devised, as is the custom in some other churches. "In order to the best effect, we need also to institute some method of introducing baptized children to the church, that is distinct and peculiar to them— such a method as will place them in the condition of can-

didates, and such as will carry an expectation that they
will come forward, at a suitable age, to assume the covenant, into which they have been entered by their parents.
. . . The Lutheran and German Reformed churches still retain a rite of confirmation. If instead of the form of in-
duction called a *profession,* we had a form of *acknowledge-
ment,* or *assumption,* in which the infant member acknowledges the initial membership, his parents gave him, and assumes the vows of dedication for himself, in which they
gave him to God, the effect would unquestionably be
great." [1]

But the defender of the faith is adamant. Such a
course would be disastrous. Again his attitude to other
denominations is outspoken. This practice has corrupted
the German and Episcopal churches and has contributed
to multitudes in these communions being deluded to their
everlasting ruin. "The effect undoubtedly would be great,
and in my opinion, most disastrous to the purity of the
churches. . . . Let baptized children be presumed to be pious
unless by outward immorality, or open hostility, they give
decisive evidence to the contrary, and let them be received
to full communion in the church on this presumption, and
without any examination in respect to their religious feelings; and it is my full conviction that it would corrupt the
church, and be the means of confirming multitudes in delusion to their everlasting ruin. That such is the effect
of confirmation as practiced in the Episcopal church, and in
the Lutheran and German Reformed churches, cannot admit
of a question." (Letter VI, ps. 69-70).

According to the genius of the time, there is no am-
biguity as to the positions of the protagonists. The issues

[1] *Views,* p. 235.

are clearly drawn. But in the whole study of Bushnell's
life and work, including these bitter controversies, one cannot get away from his gift for friendship and what must
have been the winsomeness of his personality combined with
great strength. It was because of this, in no small part,
that he won through, retaining the confidence of those who
disagreed sharply with him on doctrinal grounds. One
brief picture from near the end of his ministry may be
permitted, illustrating the hold he had on his brother ministers. At one of the last meetings, in the South Church,
he got up and said: "Brethren, I am going to read what
is probably my last sermon," and then announced his subject,—*Our Relations to Christ in the Future Life.* "We
listened with eager, tender attention," says Dr. Edwin Pond
Parker, who was present. "When he finished, there was a
long silence. No one cared or dared to speak. At length
the Doctor said,—'Come, Burton, tell us what you think of
it!' Dr. Burton hesitatingly said,—'Dr. Bushnell tells us
that this is his last sermon!' He got no farther, but bowed
his head and wept. And we all wept together. Then we
knew how we loved him, and how he loved us, and what
an irreparable loss his departure would be for us. The dear
old Doctor, calmest of all, his deep eyes full of tears, his
wan face radiant, looked on us with heavenly grace and
benediction." [1]

---

[1] Parker, Edwin Pond. *The Hartford Central Association and the
Bushnell Controversy.* ps. 26-27.

CHAPTER V

MAIN POINTS IN BUSHNELL'S THEORY
OF CHRISTIAN NURTURE

I N THE preceding chapters the genesis and growth of
Bushnell's ideas in regard to Christian nurture have
been traced and something of the controversy that
ensued has been sketched. It seems now as if after the
passing of the years, it might be well to present what seem
to be main points in Bushnell's theory of Christian Nurture.
Of course the best thing is to read his own books. Their
literary style, vivid figures of speech and progressive ideas
make them as fresh and striking, almost, as if written
today.

Many of the ideas Bushnell advances are as timely
today as they were over half a century ago. Some of these
passages might well be published as tracts for the times.
The following selections will show the main points in Christian Nurture. The quotations are all from *Views of Christian Nurture and of Subjects Adjacent Thereto,* published
by Edwin Hunt, at Hartford in 1847. [1]

DISCOURSE I [2]

"There is then some kind of nurture which is of the
Lord, deriving a quality and a power from Him, and com-

---

[1] Any striking changes in the 1861 edition entitled *Christian Nurture*
(Scribner, New York, 407 p.) will be noted. For the most part there
are only trivial differences of wording and punctuation.

[2] This section is Chapter I in the 1861 edition with the caption,
"What Christian Nurture Is".

municating the same. Being instituted by Him, it will of necessity have a method and a character peculiar to itself, or rather to Him. It will be the Lord's way of education, having aims appropriate to Him, and if realized in its full intent, terminating in results impossible to be reached by any merely human method.

"What then is the true idea of Christian, or divine nurture, as distinguished from that which is not Christian? What is its aim? What its method of working? What its powers and instruments? What its contemplated results? Few questions have greater moment, and it is one of the pleasant signs of the times, that the subject involved is beginning to attract new interest, and excite a spirit of inquiry which heretofore has not prevailed in our churches. (p. 5).

"What is the true idea of Christian education?—I answer in the following proposition, which it will be the aim of my argument to establish, viz:

THAT THE CHILD IS TO GROW UP A CHRISTIAN. [1] In other words, the aim, effort, and expectation should be, not, as is commonly assumed, that the child is to grow up in sin, to be converted after he comes to a mature age; but that he is to open on the world as one that is spiritually renewed, not remembering the time when he went through a technical experience, but seeming rather to have loved what is good from his earliest years. I do not affirm that every child may, in fact and without exception, be so trained that he certainly will grow up a Christian. . . .

"This doctrine is not a novelty, now rashly and for the first time propounded, as some of you may be tempted to suppose. I shall show you, before I have done with the ar-

---

[1] See footnote 1, p. 49.

gument, that it is as old as the Christian church, and prevails extensively at the present day, in other parts of the world. (p. 6). It is conceivable that regenerate character may exist, long before it is fully and formally developed. (p. 7).

"In pursuing the argument, I shall

I. Collect some considerations which occur to us, viewing the subject on the human side, and then—

II. Show how far and by what methods God has justified, on his part, the doctrine we maintain.

"There is then, as the subject appears to us—

1. No absurdity in supposing that children are to grow up in Christ. On the other hand, if there is no absurdity, there is a very clear moral incongruity in setting up a contrary supposition, to be the aim of a system of Christian education. There could not be a worse or more baleful implication given to a child, than that he is to reject God and all holy principle, till he has come to a mature age. What authority have you from the Scriptures to tell your child, or, by any sign, to show him that you do not expect him truly to love and obey God, till after he has spent whole years in hatred and wrong? What authority to make him feel that he is the most unprivileged of all human beings, capable of sin, but incapable of repentance; old enough to resist all good, but too young to receive any good whatever? It is reasonable to suppose that you have some express authority for a lesson so manifestly cruel and hurtful, else you would shudder to give it. I ask you for the chapter and verse, out of which it is derived. Meantime, wherein would it be less incongruous for you to teach your child that he is to lie and steal, and go the whole round of the vices and then, after he comes to mature age,

reform his conduct by the rules of virtue? Perhaps you do not give your child to expect that he is to grow up in sin, you only expect that he will yourself. That is scarcely better, for that which is your expectation, will assuredly be his. (ps. 9-10).

"But my child is a sinner, you will say, and how can I expect him to begin a right life, until God gives him a new heart? This is the common way of speaking, and I state the objection in its own phraseology, that it may recognize itself. Who then has told you that a child cannot have the new heart of which you speak? Whence do you learn that if you live the life of Christ, before him and with him, the law of the Spirit of Life may not be such as to include and quicken him also? And why should it be thought incredible that there should be some really good principle awakened in the mind of a child? For this is all that is implied in a Christian state. The Christian is one who has simply *begun* to love what is good for its own sake, and why should it be thought impossible for a child to have this love begotten in him? Take any scheme of depravity you please, there is yet nothing in it to forbid the possibility that a child should be led, in his first moral act, to cleave unto what is good and right, any more than in the first of his twentieth year. (p. 10). And what more appropriate to the doctrine of spiritual influence itself, than to believe that as the Spirit of Jehovah fills all the worlds of matter, and holds a presence of power and government in all objects, so all human souls, the infantile as well as the adult, have a nurture of the Spirit appropriate to their age and their wants? What opinion is more essentially monstrous, in fact, than that which regards the Holy Spirit as having no agency in the immature souls of children who are growing up helpless and unconscious into the perils of time? (p. 11).

"2. It is to be expected that Christian education will radically differ from that which is not Christian. Now it is the very character and mark of all unchristian education, that it brings up the child for future conversion. . . . Is then Christian education, or the nurture of the Lord, no way different from this? Or is it rather to be supposed that it will have a higher aim and a more sacred character? (p. 11).

"I am well aware of the common impression that Christian education is sufficiently distinguished by the endeavor of Christian parents to teach their children the lessons of scripture history, and the doctrines or dogmas of scripture theology. But if they are given to understand, at the same time, that these lessons can be expected to produce no fruit till they are come to a mature age, that they are to grow up still in the same character as other children do, who have no such instruction, what is this but to enforce the practical rejection of all the lessons taught them? We certainly know that much of what is called Christian nurture, only serves to make the subject of religion odious, and that, as nearly as we can discover, in exact proportion to the amount of religious teaching received. And no small share of the difficulty to be overcome afterwards, in the struggle of conversion, is created in just this way. On the other hand, you will hear, for example, of cases like the following: A young man, correctly but not religiously brought up, light and gay in his manners and thoughtless hitherto in regard to any thing of a serious nature, happens accidentally one Sunday, while his friends are gone to ride, to take down a book on the evidences of Christianity. His eye, floating over one of the pages, becomes fixed, and he is surprised to find his feelings flowing out strangely into its holy truths. He is conscious of no struggle of hostility, but a new joy dawns in his being. Henceforth, to the end of a long and useful life, he is a Christian man. The love into which he was surprised continues to flow, and he is remarkable, in the churches, all his life long, as one of the most beautiful, healthful and dignified examples of Christian piety. Now a very little mis-education, called Christian, discouraging the piety it teaches, and making enmity itself a necessary ingredient in the struggle of conversion, conversion no reality without a struggle, might have sufficed to close the mind of this man against every thought of religion to the end of life. (ps. 12-13). Something is wanted that is better than teaching, something that transcends mere effort and will-work—the loveliness of a good life, the repose of faith, the confidence of righteous expectation, the sacred and cheerful liberty of the Spirit—all glowing about the young soul, as a warm and genial nurture, and forming in it, by methods that are silent and imperceptible, a spirit of duty and religious obedience to God. This only is Christian nurture, the nurture of the Lord.

"3. It is a fact that all Christian parents would like to see their children grow up in piety; and, the better Christians they are, the more earnestly they desire it; and, the more lovely and constant the Christian spirit they manifest the more likely is it, in general, that their children will early display the Christian character. This is current opinion. But why should a Christian parent, the deeper his piety and the more closely he is drawn to God, be led to desire, the more earnestly, what, in God's view, is even absurd or impossible? And, if it be generally seen that the children of such are more likely to become Christians early, what forbids the hope that, if they were better Christians still, living a more single and Christ-like life, and more cultivated in their views of family nurture, they might not see their children grow up always in piety towards God. (p. 13).

"4. Assuming the corruption of human nature, when should we think it wisest to undertake or expect a remedy? When evil is young and pliant to good, or when it is confirmed by years of sinful habit? And when, in fact, is the human heart found to be so ductile to the motives of religion, as in the simple, ingenuous age of childhood? How easy it is then, as compared with the stubbornness of adult years, to make all wrong seem odious, all good lovely and desirable. . . . He cannot understand, of course, in the earliest stage of childhood, the philosophy of religion as a renovated experience, and that is not the form of the first lessons he is to receive. He is not to be told that he must have a new heart and exercise faith in Christ's atonement. We are to understand, that a right spirit may be virtually exercised in children, when, as yet, it is not intellectually received, or as a form of doctrine. (p. 14). Never is it too early for good to be communicated. Infancy and childhood are the ages most pliant to good. And who can think it necessary that the plastic nature of childhood must first be hardened into stone, and stiffened into enmity towards God and all duty, before it can become a candidate for Christian character! There could not be a more unnecessary mistake, and it is as unnatural and pernicious, I fear, as it is unnecessary.

"There are many who assume the radical goodness of human nature, and the work of Christian education, is, in their view, only to educate, or educe the good that is in us. Let no one be disturbed by the suspicion of a coincidence between what I have here said and such a theory. . . . View the matter as we will, there is no so unreasonable assumption, none so wide of all just philosophy, as that which proposes to form a child to virtue, by simply educing or drawing out what is in him. The growth of Christian virtue is no vegetable process, no mere onward development. It involves a struggle with evil, a fall and a rescue. (ps. 14-15). For it is not sin which he derives from his parents; at least not sin in any sense which imports blame, but only some prejudice to the perfect harmony of his mold, some kind of pravity or obliquity which inclines him to evil. These suggestions are offered, not as necessary to be received in every particular, but simply to show that the scheme of education proposed, is not to be identified with another, which assumes the radical goodness of human nature, and according to which, if it be true, Christian education is insignificant.

"5. It is implied in all our religious philosophy, that if a child ever does any thing in a right spirit, ever loves any thing because it is good and right, it involves the dawn of a new life. This we cannot deny or doubt, without bringing in question our whole scheme of doctrine. Is it then incredible that some really good feeling should be called into exercise in a child? . . . Nor is there any age, which offers itself to God's truth and love, and to that quickening spirit whence all good proceeds, with so much of ductile feeling and susceptibilities so tender. (p. 16).

"6. Children have been so trained as never to remember the time when they began to be religious. Baxter was at one time greatly troubled concerning himself, because he could recollect no time, when there was a gracious change in his character. But he discovered, at length, that 'education is as properly a means of grace as preaching', and thus found a sweeter comfort in his love to God, that he learned to love him so early. The European churches, generally, regard Christian piety more as a habit of life, formed under the training of childhood, and less as a marked spiritual change in experience. In Germany, for example, the church includes all the people, and it is re-markable that, under a scheme so loose, and with so much of pernicious error taught in the pulpit, there is yet so much of deep religious feeling, so much of lovely and simple character, and a savor of Christian piety so generally preva-lent in the community. So true is this, that the German people are every day spoken of as a people religious by nature; no other way being observed of accounting for the strong religious bent they manifest. Whereas it is due, beyond any reasonable question, to the fact that children are placed under a form of treatment which expects them to be religious, and are not discouraged by the demand of an experience above their years. Again, the Moravian Brethren, it is agreed by all, give as ripe and graceful an exhibition of piety, as any body of Christians living on the earth, and it is the radical distinction of their system that it rests its power on Christian education. They make their churches schools of holy nurture to childhood, and expect their children to grow up there, as plants in the house of the Lord. Accordingly it is affirmed that not one in ten of the members of that church, recollects any time when he began to be religious. Is it then incredible that what has been can be? Would it not be wiser and more modest, when facts are against us, to admit that there is certainly some bad error, either in our life, or in our doctrine, or in both, which it becomes us to amend?

"Once more, if we narrowly examine the relation of parent and child, we shall not fail to discover something like a law of organic connection, [1] as regards character, subsisting between them. Such a connection as makes it easy to believe, and natural to expect that the faith of the one will be propagated in the other. (ps. 17-18). It is a singular fact, that many believe substantially the same thing, in regard to evil character, but have no thought of any such possibility in regard to good. There has been much speculation, of late, as to whether a child is born in depravity, or whether the depraved character is superinduced afterwards. But, like many other great questions, it determines much less than is commonly supposed; for, according to the most proper view of the subject, a child is really not born till he emerges from the infantile state, and never before that time can be said to receive a separate and properly individual nature. (ps. 18-19). For the child, after birth, is still within the matrix of the parental life, and will be more or less, for many years. And the parental life will be flowing into him all that time, just as naturally, and by a law as truly organic, as when the sap of the trunk flows into a limb. . . . Will, in connection with conscience, is the basis of personality, or individuality, and these exist as yet only in their rudimental type, as when the form of a seed is beginning to unfold at the root of a flower. At first, the child is held as a mere passive lump in the arms, and he

---

[1] Bushnell has a footnote explaining this term, because of criticism. He shows "it is a term in common philosophic use in connection with all the great questions of government and society . . . Government is, in this view, the organic conscience of the State—no matter what may be the form, or who presides". (p. 18).

opens into conscious life under the soul of the parent
streaming into his eyes and ears, through the manners and
tones of the nursery. The kind and degree of passivity
are gradually changed as life advances. A little farther on
it is observed that a smile wakens a smile—any kind of
sentiment or passion, playing in the face of the parent,
wakens a responsive sentiment or passion. (p. 19). The
tendency of all our modern speculations is to an extreme
individualism, and we carry our doctrines of free will so
far as to make little or nothing of organic laws. . . . We
have much to say also, . . . about the beginning of moral
agency, and we seem to fancy that there is some definite
moment when a child becomes a moral agent, passing out
of a condition where he is a moral nullity, and where no
moral agency touches his being. Whereas he is rather to
be regarded at the first, as lying within the moral agency
of the parent and passing out by degrees through a course
of mixed agency, to a proper independency and self-posses-
sion. The supposition that he becomes, at some certain
moment, a complete moral agent, which a moment before
he was not, is clumsy and has no agreement with observation. The separation is gradual. He is never, at any moment after birth, to be regarded as perfectly beyond the
sphere of good and bad exercises; for the parent exercises
himself in the child, playing his emotions and sentiments,
and working a character in him, by virtue of an organic
power. And this is the very idea of Christian education,
that it begins with nurture or cultivation. And the intention is that the Christian life and spirit of the parents shall
flow into the mind of the child, to blend with his incipient
and half-formed exercises; that they shall thus beget their
own good within him, their thoughts, opinions, faith and

love, which are to become a little more, and yet a little more, his own separate exercise, but still the same in character. The contrary assumption, that virtue must be the product of separate and absolutely independent choice, is pure assumption. (ps. 20-21).

All society is organic—the church, the state, the school, the family, and there is a spirit in each of these organisms, peculiar to itself, and more or less hostile, more or less favorable to religious character, and to some extent, at least, sovereign over the individual man. A very great share of the power in what is called a revival of religion, is organic power; nor is it any the less divine on that account. The child is only more within the power of organic laws than we all are. We possess only a mixed individuality all our life long. A pure, separate, individual man, living *wholly* within, and from himself, is a mere fiction. No such person ever existed, or ever can. I need not say that this view of an organic connection of character subsisting between parent and child, lays a basis for notions of Christian education, far different from those which now prevail, under the cover of a merely fictitious and mischievous individualism.

"Perhaps it may be necessary to add, that, in the strong language I have used concerning the organic connection of character between the parent and the child, it is not designed to assert a power in the parent to renew the child, or that the child can be renewed by any agency of the Spirit less immediate, than that which renews the parent himself. When a germ is formed on the stem of any plant, the formative instinct of the plant may be said in one view to produce it; but the same solar heat which quickens the plant, must quicken also the germ and sustain the internal action of growth, by a common presence in both. So if there be an organic power of character in the parent, such as that of which I have spoken, it is not a complete power in itself, but only such a power as demands the realizing presence of the Spirit of God, both in the parent and the child, to give it effect. As Paul said, 'I have begotten you through the gospel,' so may we say of the parent, who having a living gospel enveloped in his life, brings it into organic connection with the soul of childhood. But the declaration excludes the necessity of a divine influence, not more in one case than in the other.

"Such are some of the considerations that offer themselves, viewing our subject on the human side, or as it appears in the light of human evidence—all concurring to produce the conviction, that it is the only true idea of Christion education, that the child is to grow up in the life of the parent, and be a Christian, in principle, from his earliest years." (ps. 21-22).

DISCOURSE II [1]

"We proceed now to inquire—

II. How far God, in the revelation made of his character and will, favors the view of Christian nurture already vindicated by arguments and evidences of an inferior nature? And—

1. According to all that God has taught us concerning his own dispositions, he desires, on his part, that children should grow up in piety, as earnestly as the parent can desire it; nay, as much more earnestly, as he hates sin

---

[1] This section is Chapter II in the 1861 edition with the caption "What Christian Nurture Is".

more intensely, and desires good with less mixture of qualification.   Goodness, or the production of goodness, is the
supreme end of God, and therefore we know, on first principles, that he desires to bestow whatsoever spiritual grace
is necessary to the moral renovation of childhood, and will
do it, unless some collateral reasons in his plan, involving
the extension of holy virtue, require him to withold."
(p. 23).

"2.   If there be any such thing as Christian nurture,
distinguished from that which is not Christian, which is
generally admitted, and, by the Scriptures clearly asserted,
then is it some kind of nurture which God appoints.   Does
it then, accord with the known character of God, to appoint
a scheme of education, the only proper result of which shall
be that children are trained up under it in sin?   It would
not be more absurd to suppose that God has appointed
church education, to produce a first crop of sin, and then a
crop of holiness. (p. 24).   Holy virtue is the aim of every
plan God adopts, every means he prescribes, and we have
no right to look only for sin, in that which he has appointed
as a means of virtue.   We cannot do it understandingly,
without great impiety.

"3.   God does expressly lay it upon us to expect that
our children will grow up in piety, under the parental nurture, and assumes the possibility that such a result may
ordinarily be realized.   'Train up a child'—how? for future
conversion?—No, 'but in the way he should go, that when
he is old he may not depart from it.' . . . 'Bring them up in
the nurture and admonition of the Lord,' a form of expression, which indicates the existence of a Divine nurture, that
is to encompass the child and mold him unto God; so that
he shall be brought up, as it were, in Him. (p. 25).

"4. A time is foretold, as our churches generally believe, when all shall know God, even from the least to the greatest; that is, shall spiritually know him, or so that there shall be no need of exhorting one another to know him; for intellectual knowledge is not carried by exhortation. If such a time is ever to come, then, at least, children are to grow up in Christ; can it come too soon? . . . Our very theory of religion is, that men are to grow up in evil, and be dragged into the church of God by conquest. The world is to lie in halves, and the kingdom of God is to stretch itself side by side with the kingdom of darkness, making sallies into it, and taking captive those who are sufficiently hardened and bronzed in guiltiness to be converted. . . . The Christian scheme has a scope of intention, and instruments and powers adequate to this,—it descends upon the world to claim all souls for its dominion,—all men of all climes, all ages from childhood to the grave. . . . Let us either renounce any such confidence, or show by a thorough consistency in our religious doctrines, that we hold it deliberately and manfully. (ps. 25-26).

"5. We discover in the Scriptures that the organic law of which I have spoken, is distinctly recognized, and that character, in children, is often regarded as, in some very important sense, derivative from their parents. 'The unfeigned faith, which dwelt first, in thy grandmother Lois, and thy mother Eunice, and, I am persuaded that in thee also.' Not that in the bald and naked sense, it had descended thus through three generations. . . . In like manner, God is represented as 'keeping covenant and mercy with them that love him and keep his commandments, to a thousand generations'; which, if it signifies any thing, amounts to a declaration that he will spiritually own and bless every succeeding generation, to the end of the world, if only the preceding one will so live as to be fit vehicles of his blessing; for it is not any covenant, as a form of mutual contract, which carries the Divine favor, but it is the loving Him rather, and keeping His commandments, by an upright, godly life, which sets the parents on terms of friendship with God, and secures the inhabitation of His power. (ps. 26-27).

"The Scriptures have a perpetual habit, if I may so speak, of associating children with the character and destiny of their parents. In this respect, they maintain a marked contrast with the extreme individualism of our modern philosophy. They do not always regard the individual as an isolated unit, but they often look upon men as they exist, in families and races, and under organic laws." (ps. 27-28).

"Last argument, which is drawn from infant or household baptism— a rite which supposes the fact of an organic connection of character between the parent and the child; a seal of faith in the parent, applied over to the child, on the ground of a presumption that his faith is wrapped up in the parent's faith; so that he is accounted a believer from the beginning. . . . Furthermore you will perceive that it must be presumed, either that the child will grow up a believer, or that he will not. God presumes that he will, and therefore appoints it.

"It was taken for granted, as a matter of common understanding, that, in a change of religion, the children went with the parents,—if they became Jews that their children would be Jews, if Christian believers that their children would be Christians. (p. 30).

"The Jewish nation regarded other nations as unclean. Hence, when a Gentile family wished to become Jewish citizens, they were baptized in token of cleansing. Then they were said to be re-born, or regenerated, so as to be accounted true descendants of Abraham. We use the term *naturalize,* that is to *make natural born,* in the same sense. (ps. 30-31). Some have questioned whether proselyte baptism existed at this early age; but of this, the third chapter of John is itself conclusive proof; for how else was baptism familiarly known to the Jews as connected with regeneration; that is, civil regeneration? . . . In this manner, all his language, in the interview with Nicodemus, becomes natural and easy. (p. 31).

"Then passing into the early history of the church, we hear Justin Martyr, saying,—'there are some of us, eighty years old, who were made disciples to Christ in their childhood,' that is, in the age of the apostles, and while they were yet living; for it was now less than eighty years since their death.

"Then again, Irenæus, who lived within one generation of the apostles, gives us the second mention of this rite which appears in history, when he says, 'Christ came to save all persons through himself; all I say, who through him are regenerated unto God; infants and little ones, and children and youth, and the aged.' (p. 32).

"You perceive too, in this exposition, that the view of Christian nurture I am endeavoring to vindicate, is not new, but is older, by far, than the one now prevalent,—as old as the Christian church. (ps. 32-33).

"In this way too is it seen that the Christian economy has a place for all ages; for it would be singular, if after all we say of the universality of God's mercy as a gift to the human race, it could yet not limber itself to man, so as to adapt a place for the age of childhood, but must leave a full fourth part of the race, the part least hardened in evil and tenderest to good unrecognized and unprovided for,—gathering a flock without lambs, or, I should rather say, gathering a flock away from the lambs. Such is not the spirit of Him who said, 'forbid them not, for of such is the kingdom of heaven.' (ps. 33-34).

"1. A theoretical objection that it leaves no room for the sovereignty of God, in appointing the moral character of men and families. Thus it is declared that 'all are not Israel who are of Israel,' and that God, before the children Jacob and Esau had done either good or evil, professed his love to one, and his rejection of the other. But the wonder is, in this case of Rebecca and her children, that such a mother did not ruin them both. A partial mother, scorning one child, teaching the other to lie and trick his blind father, and extort from a starving brother his birthright honor, cannot be said to furnish a very good test of the power of Christian education. . . . The sovereignty of God has always a relation to means, and we are not authorized to think of it, in any case, as separated from means. (ps. 34-35).

"2. An objection from observation,—asking why it is, if our doctrine be true, that many persons, remarkable for their piety, have yet been so unfortunate in their children? Because, I answer, many persons, remarkable for their piety, are yet very disagreeable persons, and that too, by reason of some very marked defect in their religious character. They display just that spirit, and act in just that manner, which is likely to make religion odious,—the more odious the more urgently they commend it. Sometimes they appear well to the world one remove distant from them, they shine well in their written biography, but one living in their family will know what others do not; and if their children turn out badly, will never be at a loss for the reason. Many persons too have such defective views of the manner of teaching appropriate to early childhood, that they really discourage their children. (p. 35).

"I once took up a book, from a Sabbath school library, one problem of which was to teach a child that he wants a new heart. A lovely boy (for it was a narrative) was called every day, to resolve that he would do no wrong that day, a task which he undertook most cheerfully, at first, and even with a show of delight. But, before the sun went down, he was sure to fall into some ill-temper or be overtaken by some infirmity. Whereupon, the conclusion was immediately sprung upon him that he wanted a new heart. We are even amazed that any teacher of ordinary intelligence should not once have imagined how she herself, or how the holiest Christian living would fare under such kind of regimen; how certain to discover every day, and probably some hours before sunset, that she too wanted a new heart. And the practical cruelty of the experiment is yet more to be deplored, than its want of consideration. Had the problem been how to discourage most effectually every ingenuous struggle of childhood, no readier or surer method could have been devised. (ps. 35-36).

"First, he cannot guess what this technical phraseology means, and thus he takes up the impression that he can do, or think nothing right, till he is able to comprehend what is above his age—why then should he make the endeavor? Secondly, he is told that he must have a new heart *before* he can be good, not that he may hope to exercise a renewed spirit, *in* the endeavor to be good—why then attempt what must be worthless, till something *previous* befalls him? Discouraged thus on every side, his tender soul turns hither and thither, in hopeless despair, and finally he consents to be what he must—a sinner against God and that only. Well is it, under such a process, wearing down his childish soul into soreness and despair of good, sealing up his nature in silence and cessation as regards all right endeavors, and compelling him to turn his feelings into other channels, where he shall find his good in evil— well is it, I say, if he has not contracted a dislike to the very subject of religion, as inveterate as the subject is impossible. (p. 36). . . . Rather should they begin with a kind of teaching suited to the age of the child. First of all, they should rather seek to teach a feeling than a doctrine, to bathe the child in their own feeling of love to God, and dependence on him, and contrition for wrong before him, bearing up their child's heart in their own, not fearing to encourage every good motion they can call into exercise; to make what is good, happy and attractive; what is wrong, odious and hateful. Then as the understanding advances, give it food suited to its capacity, opening upon it, gradually, the more difficult views of Christian doctrine and experience.

"Sometimes Christian parents fail of success in the religious training of their children, because the church counteracts their effort and example. The church makes a bad atmosphere about the house and the poison comes in at the doors and windows. It is rent by divisions, burnt up by fanaticism, frozen by the chill of a worldly spirit, petrified in a rigid and dead orthodoxy. It makes no element of genial warmth and love about the child, according

to the intention of Christ in its appointment, but gives to
religion, rather a forbidding aspect, and thus, instead of
assisting the parent, becomes one of the worst impediments
to his success. (ps. 36-37).

"To sum up all, we conclude, not that every child can
certainly be made to grow up in Christian piety—nothing
is gained by asserting so much, and perhaps I could not
prove it to be true, neither can any one prove the contrary—
I merely show that this is the true idea and aim of Christian nurture as a nurture of the Lord. It is presumptively
true that such a result can be realized, just as it is presumptively true that a school will forward the pupils in knowledge, though possibly sometimes it may fail to do it. And,
without such a presumption, no parent can do his duty and
fill his office well, any more than it is possible to make a
good school, in the expectation that the scholars will learn
something five or ten years hence and not before. (ps.
37-38).

"To give this subject its practical effect, let me
urge it—

"1. Upon the careful attention of those who neglect,
or decline, offering their children in baptism. Some of you
are simply indifferent to this duty, not seeing what good it
can do to baptize a child; others have positive theological
objections to it. With the former class I certainly agree,
so far as to admit that baptism, as an operation, can do no
good to your child; but, if it has no importance in what it
operates, it has the greatest importance in what it signifies.
(p. 38). . . . If children are to grow up in sin, to be converted when they come to the age of maturity, if this is the
only aim and expectation of family nurture, there really is
no meaning or dignity whatever in the rite. . . . And it

would certainly be very singular, if Christ Jesus, in a scheme of mercy for the world, had found no place for infants and little children; more singular still if he had given them the place of adults; and worse than singular, if he had appointed them to years of sin as the necessary preparation for his mercy. . . . And is it for you to withhold them from that place? Is it worthy of your tenderness, as a Christian parent, to leave them outside of the fold, when the gate is open, only taking care to go in yourself? . . . What can be worse, what can make them aliens more sensibly from Christ's sympathies, what can more effectually discourage and chill them to all thought of a good life, than to make them feel that Christ has no place for them, till their sins are ripe, and they are capable of a grace that is now above their years? What more persuasive, than to know that he has taken them into his school already, to grow up round him as disciples? (ps. 39-40). Once more I ask you to consider whether God is not better to you than you yourselves have thought, and whether, in withholding your children from God, you are not like to fall as far short of your duty as you do of the privilege offered you. (ps. 40-41).

"2. What motives are laid upon all Christian parents, by the doctrine I have established, to make the first article of family discipline a constant and careful discipline of themselves. I would not undervalue a strong and decided government in families. No family can be rightly trained without it. But there is a kind of virtue, my brethren, which is not in the rod, the virtue, I mean, of a truly good and sanctified life. And a reign of brute force is much more easily maintained, than a reign whose power is righteousness and love. There are too, I must warn you, many

who talk much of the rod as the orthodox symbol of parental duty, but who might really as well be heathens as
Christians; who only storm about their house with heathen-
ish ferocity, who lecture, and threaten, and castigate, and
bruise, and call this family government. They even dare
to speak of this as the nurture of the Lord. So much easier
is it to be violent than to be holy, that they substitute force
for goodness and grace, and are wholly unconscious of the
imposture. It is frightful to think how they batter and
bruise the delicate, tender souls of their children, extin-
guishing in them what they ought to cultivate, crushing
that sensibility which is the hope of their being, and all in
the sacred name of Christ Jesus. By no such summary
process can you dispatch your duties to your children. You
are not to be a savage to them, but a father, and a Christian. Your real aim and study must be to infuse into them
a new life, and, to this end, the Life of God must perpetually reign in you. . . . It must be seen and felt with them
that religion is a first thing with you. And it must be first,
not in words and talk, but visibly first in your love—that
which fixes your aims, feeds your enjoyments, sanctifies
your pleasures, supports your trials, satisfies your wants,
contents your ambition, beautifies and blesses your character. No mock piety, no sanctimony of phrase, or longitude
of face on Sundays will suffice. You must live in the light
of God and hold such a spirit in exercise, as you wish to
see translated into your children. (ps. 41-42). This is
Christian education, the nurture of the Lord. Ah, how
dismal is the contrast of a half-worldly, carnal piety, pro-
posing money as the good thing of life, stimulating ambition for place and show, provoking ill-nature by petulance
and falsehood, praying to save the rule of family worship,

having now and then a religious fit, and, when it is on, weeping and exhorting the family to undo all that the life has taught them to do, and then, when the passions have burnt out their fire, dropping down again to sleep in the cinders, only hoping still that the family will sometime be converted! When shall we discover that families ought to be ruined by such training as this? When shall we turn ourselves wholly to God, and looking on our children as one with us and drawing their character from us, make them arguments to duty and constancy—duty and constancy not as a burden, but since they are enforced by motives so dear, our pleasure and delight. (p. 42). Hence it is that monks have been so prone to persecution. Not dwelling with children as the objects of affection, having their hearts softened by no family love, their life identified with no objects that excite gentleness, their nature hardens into a Christian abstraction, and blood and doctrine go together. (ps. 42-43).

"3. We have been expecting to thrive too much by conquest, and too little by growth. I desire to speak with all caution of what are very unfortunately called revivals of religion. (p. 43). But the difficulty is with us that we idolize such scenes and make them the whole of our religion. We assume that nothing good is doing, or can be done at any other time. And what is even worse, we often look upon these scenes, and desire them, rather as scenes of victory, than of piety. They are the harvest times of conversion, and conversion is too nearly every thing with us. In particular, we see no way to gather in disciples, save by means of certain marked experiences, developed in such scenes, in adult years. Our very children can possibly come to no good, save in this way. Instrumentalities are invented

to compass our object, that are only mechanical, and the
hope of mere present effect is supposed to justify them.
Present effect, in the view of many, justifies any thing and
every thing. We strain every nerve of motion, exhaust
every capacity of endurance, and push on till nature sinks
in exhaustion. We preach too much, and live Christ too
little. We do many things, which in a cooler mood, are
seen to hurt the dignity of religion, and which somewhat
shame and sicken ourselves. Hence the present state of
religion in our country. We have worked a vein till it has
run out. The churches are exhausted. . . . Nothing different
from this ought to have been expected. No nation can long
thrive by a spirit of conquest; no more can a church.
There must be an internal growth, that is made by holy
industry, in the common walks of life and duty. Let us
turn now, not away from revivals of religion, certainly not
away from the conviction that God will bring upon the
churches tides of spiritual exercise, and vary his divine culture by times and seasons suited to their advancement; but
let us turn to inquire whether there is not a fund of increase in the very bosom of the church itself. Let us try
if we may not train up our children in the way that they
should go. Simply this, if we can do it, will make the
churches multiply her numbers many fold more rapidly
than now with the advantage that many more will be gained
from without than now. . . . Her piety will be of a more
even and genial quality, and will be more respected. She
will not strive and cry, but she will live. The school of
John the Baptist will be succeeded by the school of Christ,
as a dew comes after a fire (ps. 44-45). Then also the
piety of the coming age will be deeper and more akin to
habit than yours, because it was begun earlier. . . . Not

born so generally, in a storm, and brought to Christ by an abrupt transition, the latter portion of life will not have an unequal war to maintain with the beginning, but life will be more nearly one, and in harmony with itself. Is not this a result to be desired? Could we tell our American churches at this moment, what they want, should we not tell them this? . . . Religion never thoroughly penetrates life, till it becomes domestic. Like that patriotic fire, which makes a nation invincible, it never burns with inextinguishable devotion, till it burns at the hearth. (ps. 45-46).

"4. Parents who are not religious in their character, have reason, in our subject, seriously to consider what effect they are producing, and likely to produce in their children. Probably you do not wish them to be irreligious. . . . But, alas! how difficult is it for you to convince them, by words, of the value of what you practically reject yourselves. . . . What then are they daily deriving from you? but that which you yourselves reveal, in your prayerless house, and at your thankless table? (p. 46). Do not imagine that you have done corrupting them, when they are born. Their character is yet to be born, and, in you, is to have its parentage." (ps. 46-47).

This concludes the presentation of some of the main ideas in Bushnell's theory of Christian nurture. The next enquiry is to what extent these are accepted today. It is amazing to find the degree to which they are accepted as basic principles in teaching religion nearly one hundred years after they were written.

CHAPTER VI

BUSHNELL AND RELIGIOUS EDUCATION TODAY

THERE is no doubt that religious education, the out-standing movement in the church in this century, finds itself in harmony with Bushnell's spirit and teaching. Almost every student of Bushnell emphasizes his preeminence as preacher, writer and citizen, but some of them seem unaware that his most revolutionary influence was in religious education.

It is very easy to overstate the contributions of a great teacher and writer by reading into his words meanings that were not intended but which have become commonplaces in the intervening years. This is eminently true of inter-pretations of great literature like the Bible and the plays of Shakespeare. There is no desire to do this in the present instance, if for no other reason than that religious educa-tion has made great strides both in theory and practice during recent years.

At the outset it should be made clear that Bushnell was not familiar with educational techniques. He was a prophet and preacher who saw certain fundamental ideas clearly without always realizing their full implication. Philip E. Howard said of him "For Horace Bushnell was nothing less than that,—a prophet of vision, whose philosophical, specu-lative, discerning mind gained an independent grasp of

spiritual truth by daring exploration. . . ." [1]   Yet Bushnell tried to get Trumbull out of Sunday school work and
into the pastorate, and presented to him invitations to
prominent churches.   This shows that Bushnell did not
value religious education at its true worth.   But he had
the discrimination later to see his mistake and the bigness
and courage to admit it.   In spite of his influence Trumbull
continued to give his life to the Sunday School.   "Trumbull," said Bushnell later, "you knew better than I did
where the Lord wanted you.   I honestly thought the pulpit
was a bigger place for you, and I tried to get you into it.
But now I've come to see that the work you are doing is the
greatest work in the world." (p. 259).

But ideas for which Bushnell stood are now so taken
for granted that it is difficult to appreciate the situation
nearly one hundred years ago.   The controversy reveals
some of it.   Revivalism was rampant and it was considered
essential even for tiny children to have the conviction of
sin, a mighty inner struggle, and a sense of conversion and
assurance, as well as for the adult who had grossly sinned.
It will be recalled that Tyler scorned the idea that any one
should become a Christian without this struggle.

In attempting to show something of the relationship
between Bushnell and present-day religious education, it is,
of course, impossible to refer to any large proportion of the
leaders or to follow many trends.   Considering the whole
field, it seems well to give some attention to the following
movements: The Young People's Society of Christian Endeavor; Organized Sunday School Work; The Religious
Education Association; Modern Missions; and the Pro-

[1] Howard, Philip E.   *The Life Story of Henry Clay Trumbull*, Philadelphia, The Sunday School Times, 1905.   p. 255.

gressive Education Association. It will also be necessary
to consider a few of the main conceptions of Bushnell in
relation to the work today.

1. One of the most vital movements in the church in
the last half century was the Young People's Society of
Christian Endeavor, organized by the Rev. Francis E.
Clark. It appealed to the imagination of youth, stirred
their hearts, and enlisted them by the thousand in consecrated and active life "for Christ and the Church". It
came like the breath of spring to many communities and
literally brought back to life many churches—though too
often they were opposed to it. It was, in a sense, the spirit
of youth, protesting against being cribbed, cabined, confined; and it bodied itself forth in activities and expressions
suitable to its own nature. It may now have fulfilled its
function but a true interpretation of the past would probably show that it was one of the very important factors in
preparing the ground for modern religious education.

Much of Dr. Clark's thought springs naturally from
Bushnell's *Christian Nurture*, and he gladly acknowledges
this indebtedness. In his little book, *The Children and the
Church, and the Young People's Society of Christian Endeavor, as a Means of Bringing Them Together*, Dr. Clark
says: "A religious life, a life of faith and prayer, a Christ-
like life, is natural for a child, and we make a woeful mistake when we think that there is a certain amount of boyish
wickedness and girlish frivolity which must be run through
before the religious life can begin. . . . We expect to find
fragrance in the bud and purity in the mountain rill; we
should expect to find religious fragrance and purity in the
child's life. . . . We should look for it, plan for it, and be
alarmed if we do not find it; and regard a young soul with-

out it as a distorted and ill-proportioned object, a soul that lacks its chief excellence, just as a scentless bud or a brackish mountain brook would be regarded. But this early religious life, we must remember, does not take care of itself, any more than a rosebud springs up out of the ground without care; the soil must be prepared, the seed must be dropped, the little plant must be watered and nourished and pruned and trained. [1]

" . . . This was the way Samuel was trained, and David and John and Timothy. It depends upon the parents and teachers of today what the next generation shall be, and it depends upon what they do and teach to-day.

"Again, *child life in the Bible is always represented as a constant growth.*

"Over and over again we are told the child Samuel grew before the Lord. 'And Samuel grew, and the Lord was with him.' Of John the Baptist as a child it is said, 'He grew and waxed strong in spirit.' And even of our Lord Himself the same words are used. How we should shrink from using such an expression if we had no inspired authority for it! The Saviour grew, increased in spiritual power! . . . This idea is universal throughout the Bible. To become religious does not make a prodigy of a boy or girl. It does not ripen and mature the character all at once. It is not a hotbed process. . . .

"We think there is a lesson of vast importance in these considerations of child life in the Bible. . . . It is natural, it is possible, it is desirable for children to grow up into Christian manhood and womanhood without experiencing any sharp and sudden transition from an evil life to a good

[1] 3d ed.; revised and enlarged. Boston, Congregational Sunday School and Publishing Society, 1882. ps. 8-9.

life. Nay, it is not only possible and desirable, it is the
thing we ought to expect; it ought to be as common for
young children to be born into the kingdom of God as to
be born into the world."

He goes on to ask the question: "Is there a place in
the church for children?" and answers emphatically: *"The
very nature of childhood teaches us that there is a place
for children in the church"* and adds that *"the very nature
of the church proves that there ought to be a place for children within it."*

In the face of the slow growth of the churches some,
he says, exclaim: "Oh, well, it is all right, one of these
days we will have a great revival." But he goes on to
say that "Even Napoleon, king of conquest though he was,
was wiser than this. Though he laid every nation under
tribute to France, his constant principle was, France must
depend upon the children born upon her soil for her
strength and glory, rather than upon the annexation of
alien nations." He continues: " 'No nation can long thrive
by a spirit of conquest,' says Bushnell; 'no more can a
church. There must be internal growth.' " (ps. 10-29).

In addition Clark also acknowledged Bushnell in the
"Prefatory" (p. vi), and Henry Clay Trumbull in his *Yale
Lectures* points out this dependence. He shows that Clark's
aim was "to make child religion a natural, rational, perma-
ent part of the child's life." [1] If *Christian Nurture* had
done nothing more than stimulate the Christian Endeavor
movement it would have had an exceptionally rich ministry.

---

[1] *Yale Lectures on the Sunday-School.* The sunday-school; its origin,
mission, methods, and auxiliaries. The Lyman Beecher lectures before Yale Divinity School for 1888. Philadelphia, Wattles, 1888. p. 296.

2.   Turning next to an examination of a few of the great Sunday School leaders of those days Bushnell's influence in shaping their thought is seen to be direct and formative.

The Rev. Amos S. Chesebrough came under the personal magnetism of Bushnell. As Criticus Criticorum, already referred to, he did valiant service in his defense in the controversy over *Christian Nurture*. He issued a little volume entitled *Children Trained for Discipleship; Arguments and Suggestions for the Consideration of Pastors, and Christian Parents and Teachers.* [1] The opening paragraph and many other sections reveal the direct influence of Bushnell, an obligation he was always proud to acknowledge. He says: "A question whose solution is worthy of being earnestly sought is this—*Can a practicable system of religious teaching be proposed by which the successive classes of children growing up under a Pastor's charge may be so trained that they may be reasonably expected, in their early years, to enter consciously upon the Christian life and to become fitly qualified for church membership?"* (p. 7).

After taking up the objections ministers make, he adds: "No agency is too costly, no talents are of too high an order to be subsidized for this work, if needed to render it successful" and proceeds to emphasize the home life. As to revivals he says: "Whatever may be said in favor of special revival agencies . . . has no applicability to the case of children. . . . And a piety cultivated under the quiet and unforced training of the Christian Home, or of the Sunday-School, and crowned by the discriminating teachings of the Pastor, cannot but be more intelligent, health-

---

[1] New York, Anson D. F. Randolph and Co., 1883.

ful, and better balanced than a piety formed under the
powerful stimulus of revival scenes." (ps. 16 and 23).

Religious education is the pastor's duty. This he puts
in capitals: "FOR BE IT NEVER FORGOTTEN, THAT
IN THE DIVINE PLAN, THE CULTURE OF CHILD-
PIETY STANDS FIRST IN IMPORTANCE IN FUR-
NISHING THE MATERIALS OUT OF WHICH THE
CHURCH, GOD'S SPIRITUAL TEMPLE, IS TO BE
BUILT UP IN THE WORLD." (p. 41).

Chesebrough did not only profess; he practiced. As a
minister he delighted in teaching and training the young.
Trumbull in his *Yale Lectures* says Chesebrough, when
preaching, realizes he is talking to people who have heard
the gospel for years and some are as unmoved as "an im-
pregnable castle wall." Then he quotes from Chesebrough's
"The Culture of Child Piety", " 'I go now from my pulpit
into my children's training class. What a change! Every
eye glistens with attention and responsive interest. The
eager, hungry souls feed on the living bread. The plastic
characters yield to the moulding hands of truth and love.'
And I cry out, 'Oh! that those men and women who have
encased their hearts in an adamant of a third or a half
(of a) century of unbelief could have been subject to a dis-
creet and faithful Christain training in childhood! It
might not have been with them as it is now.' " (ps. 299-
300).

Trumbull, advocating the truth that the child can
know God, quotes from Bushnell's sermon, "God's Thoughts
Fit Bread for Children": "And grand Dr. Bushnell gives
added emphasis to this great truth, when he rebukes the
prevailing assumption that children are not capable of
knowing God in childhood. 'The true knowledge of God,

as in friendship,' it is assumed, he says, 'is possible to adults, but not to children; whereas the real fact is, that children are a great deal more capable of it. . . . These children can make room for more gospel than we, and take in all most precious thoughts of God more easily. The very highest and most spiritual things are a great deal closer to them than to us. Let us not wonder, and not be offended, if they break out in hosannas on just looking in the face of Jesus, when the great multitude of priests and apostles are dumb, along the road, as the ass on which he rides.'" (p. 219).

Trumbull quotes Dr. Constans L. Goodell's *How to Build a Church* (p. 35): "He who builds the Church of Christ must save the children. If we save the children, we save the world. The world is most easily and effectively saved in childhood. . . . Life and death are in the training of children. The generation which takes the most children along with it for Christ will do most to build his kingdom, and to thin the ranks of the opposition. . . . Shepherds increase their flocks by carefully nursing the lambs; so pastors enlarge their folds by caring for the young. . . . Seek the children early, seek them faithfully. The pastor's best work will be in giving direction to their life at the start." (ps. 264-265). He continues, "A unique characteristic of the Christian religion as disclosed by its divine Founder, is its exaltation of childhood. . . . The extension, the upbuilding, and the establishing of Christ's Church, must, in the plan of God, be done chiefly by means of work among and with and for the children." (ps. 374 and 377).

Trumbull deplores the habits of listlessness and inattention developed by children in the ordinary service, making the church "a place of undeserved penance to chil-

dren . . . as we know was the case prior to the introduction
of the Sunday-school." (ps. 314-315). He reports the interesting plan of the Rev. Dr. Thomas H. Gallaudet of Hartford. "He allowed them to take seats on the crickets, or
footstools, in the family pew at church; there to read their
Bibles or their Sunday-school books, while the service went
on; and, as occasion offered, he would call them up to listen
to the singing, or to a portion of Bible reading, or to some
statement or illustration in the preacher's discourse, which
was within the scope of their comprehension. In this way
. . . (the) children . . . became intelligent sharers in the
forms and spirit of sanctuary services." (p. 314).

Trumbull wishes to go much farther and makes the
revolutionary proposal that there should be something in
the whole service, (including sermon, worship and song),
suited to the children; and in this he finds his greatest inspiration in Bushnell. In his address before the Connecticut State Sunday School Convention at Hartford, in 1869,
entitled, "God's Thoughts Fit Bread for Children", Bushnell says: "Is it not our privilege and duty, as preachers
of Christ to do more preaching to children? . . . We get
occupied with great and high subjects that require a hand-
ling too heavy and deep for children, and become so fooled
in our estimate of what we do, that we call it coming down
when we undertake to preach to children; whereas it is
coming up, rather, out of the subterranean hells, dark-
nesses, intricacies, dungeon-like profundities of grown-up
sin, to speak to the bright daylight creatures of trust and
sweet affinities and easy convictions. . . . We do not preach
well to adults, because we do not preach, or learn how to
preach, to children. . . . We dry up in this manner, and our
thought wizens in a certain pomp of pretense that is hollow,

and not gospel. The very certain fact is, that our schools of theology will never make qualified preachers till they discover the existence of children." (ps. 341-342). This was spoken long before theological seminaries gave any consideration to religious education.

Samuel B. Haslett, who was one of the first to make a systematic study of the Sunday School curriculum, says: "The ideal method is for the child to grow up and develop through proper environment and instruction and training into a religious experience and life more and more advanced with the years and for the most part unconscious." In the bibliography he lists *Christian Nurture* with this annotation: "Still modern in its conception. The child is to grow into a religious character without ever knowing himself to be anything else." [1]

Philip E. Howard, Trumbull's biographer, quotes his ascription of "disciple-love" to Bushnell: "Only the superior lover of Christ and of his fellows can recognize in a young worker indications of promise that are worthy of cultivation and development. And therefore it is that such a man as Horace Bushnell incidentally does so much in bringing out and bringing up men whom a lesser man would never have deemed worthy of special notice and effort at training." [2] Trumbull said that his first acquaintance with Dr. Bushnell "was a new starting point in my religious life, to which I ever look back gratefully." (p. 256). He led him out from "dead literalism" into larger liberty.

---

[1] *The Pedagogical Bible School.* A Scientific study of the Sunday school with chief reference to the curriculum. Fleming H. Revell & Co., New York, 1903. p. 351.

[2] *The Life Story of Henry Clay Trumbull.* Philadelphia, the Sunday School Times Co., 1905. p. 255.

Only one other of the great Sunday School leaders of that day can be mentioned. Dr. John H. Vincent, later Bishop Vincent, is one of the major planets in that system. Students of the movement recognize what he owed to Bushnell. His most recent biographer is content with this note: "Could we know what thinkers had, in his opinion, most influenced him in the course of his development it would be of advantage. There were five or six to whom he felt greatly indebted. Had he written down their names it is possible that that of Chalmers might have stood at the head of the list. He constantly refers to Maurice, Bushnell, and Robertson. All were exponents in one way or another of liberalism." [1]

These brief references must suffice to indicate Bushnell's influence on the great Sunday School leaders of his day. Since the Association has developed into the International Council of Religious Education it has more frankly adopted this philosophy. The writers mentioned in the following paragraphs are members of the International Council also, or are working in co-operation with it.

3. For some years before the close of the nineteenth century there were many in the church who felt that the Sunday School was not keeping up with the times and that there was a call for new and vigorous thought and action if progress was to be made. This feeling was not confined to any one church, but was rather characteristic of leaders in most of the churches. The idea was conceived of getting people of all denominations and faiths together into an organization, the sole aim and purpose of which should be to promote the best type of religious education. This end

---

[1] Vincent, Leon H. *John Heyl Vincent.* A Biographical Sketch. New York, The Macmillan Co., 1925. p. 264.

was realized in 1903 when the organization was consum-
mated of the Religious Education Association. [1]

The Association represented the more progressive
groups in religious and in public education. Reading
through the papers and reports one cannot but be struck
by their similarity in general spirit and outlook to the
teaching of Bushnell. He is often referred to and quoted.
It will be possible to indicate but a sampling here and there
from the earliest reports to show how the progressive development was foreshadowed in his thought. The Association in itself represented that co-operation among the
denominations (including the Unitarian [2]) for which Bushnell pleaded. [3]

Francis E. Clark was true to the spirit of Bushnell
when he said, "Is it sufficient for the pastor to say: 'I am
too busy for the Sunday school, too preoccupied for young
people's work; I cannot bother mystelf about the children?'
'The young people's society is a very small part of a minister's concern,' said a pastor the other day with an impatient shrug, when urged to go occasionally to his young
people's meeting; and many a minister and Christian
worker who does not own his belief so frankly, practices
the same indifference." Then he asks: "But what is more
important? Let me ask, with all the earnestness I may
command . . . Is the Greek Testament as imperative as the
spotless page of the child's soul? Is the morning discourse
the matter of supreme importance? Is it more important
to preach to the sermon-steeped saints who little need ser-

---

[1] Proceedings of the First Annual Convention, Chicago, February 10-
12, 1903. Chicago, Executive Office of the Association.

[2] See Tyler's position, ps. 67-68.

[3] Ps. 33-34.

mons, or to sermon-hardened sinners who will not hear
them, and from whose well-fortified consciences the truth
will rebound like the cannon balls from the steel skin of
a monitor? Is the mid-week meeting of the church to be
elaborately prepared for and never missed, while the young
people's meeting is neglected? Shall we spend all our time
appealing to the minds, wills, and emotions of the aged
and middle-aged, and forget the virgin gold-mine of youth-
ful love and enthusiasm, which will so richly reward one's
toil?

"The minister or Christian worker who is too busy or
too preoccupied to care for the youth in the Sunday school
and young people's society is too busy to build up his
church." (ps. 15-16).

Professor George Albert Coe was a far-sighted and
inspiring leader and the philosopher and trusted guide of
the whole movement. He is no mere "pedisequus" of Bushnell, but he is true to his spirit. At this 1903 Convention
he sets in clear antithesis the newer and older theories of
religious teaching. "The central fact of the modern educational movement is recognition of the child as a deter-
mining factor in the whole educational scheme. The child
is a living organism, a being that grows from within by
assimilation, not from without by accretion. . . . Education
is not to press the child into any prearranged mold, but to
bring out his normal powers in their own natural order.

"Religious education has commonly proceeded from the
opposite point of view, namely, from a fixed system of religion to which the child is to be shaped."

He concludes his address with the keynote of Bushnell's *Christian Nurture:* "We must never regard either
home or church as normally successful until it is no longer

the exception but the rule for children to 'grow up Christians, and never to know themselves as being otherwise.' " (ps. 45 and 52).

Edwin D. Starbuck leaves no doubt as to where he stands. "Our work is like that of the gardener—to tend, and cultivate, and watch; if it is a rose, to try to produce the most beautiful rose; if it is a lily, then make it a perfect lily." (p. 57). And he pleads for religious teaching that suits the stage of development of the person.

John Dewey opposes "the habit of basing religious instruction upon a formulated statement of the doctrines and beliefs of the church," and advocates "bringing the child to appreciate the truly religious aspects of his own growing life," and not "inoculating him externally with beliefs and emotions which adults happen to have found serviceable to themselves." (p. 61).

Henry Churchill King says: "The religious life is primarily for a child a call to do the right thing. . . . The one imperative thing, then, for the child is to bring him into a genuine religious life of his own." (p. 77).

William P. Merrill says: "A prime characteristic of the modern conception of religious education is the increased emphasis on personality, both as object and as means. . . . To him (Jesus) the supreme power in religious training was not a speaker arousing emotion in a crowd, nor a teacher imparting knowledge to a pupil, but a spirit wakening life in another spirit." (p. 104).

President George B. Stewart's emphasis on the home is reminiscent of Bushnell. He believes that the family altar "has an incalculable and incomparable result in the religious nurture of the children. . . . The imperative obligation to make religious education in the home real, vital, potent, rests upon parents in the first instance and then upon us all." (ps. 113-114).

Nehemiah Boynton begins his address thus: "More than half a century ago Horace Bushnell declared: 'Brethren, whether you will believe it or not, a new day has come. If we will, we can make it a better day; but it demands a furniture of thought and feeling such as we must stretch ourselves in a degree to realize.'" (p. 156).

Washington Gladden in a series of lectures delivered in Boston in 1903, in an address entitled "Horace Bushnell and Progressive Orthodoxy", classifies him as a prophet especially because of his theory of Christian nurture and also because, in his aim to get rid of immoralities of theology he valiantly "battled for a 'right God.'" [1]

The tenor of the address of President William P. Faunce at the Convention in 1904 was this: "The center of studies is for us the nature of the child, made in the image of God, and revealing God at every stage of its growth." [2] And Professor Edward P. St. John conceived of religious education in the spirit of Bushnell—"this ideal for religious education does not forget God or minimize the power or part of His Spirit in the shaping of religious character. . . . To the Christian the laws of nature are the thoughts of God." (p. 248).

The passing years serve to make still more emphatic the truth in the statement of Frank Knight Sanders, president of the Religious Education Association, who asserted

---

[1] *Pioneers of Religious Liberty in America.* Being the Great and Thurston Lectures delivered in Boston in Nineteen Hundred and Three. Boston, American Unitarian Association, 1903. Chapter VII.

[2] Proceedings of the Second Annual Convention of the Religious Education Association, Philadelphia, March 2-4, 1904. p. 77.

that "It was a tremendous step forward in religious education when the idea of Christian nurture began to supersede the idea that a child must be born into the Kingdom of Heaven with some sort of spiritual convulsion." [1]

The principles enunciated in the first years of the Association have been expanded but have remained true to the spirit of these earlier statements. More recent positions are represented best in what is known as progressive or creative education, to distinguish it from the more formal and orthodox type, and it will be considered later. [2]

"His book *'Christian Nurture'* is a prophetic book, says Dr. Archibald, "for we build today, in all our ideal forms of a social order, on the foundation which he declared; and that foundation is the potential good in human nature. In every individual is the possibility inherent in the fact that every child is a child of God. And the ideal life is this: That potential good is to grow, in wisdom, in stature, and in favor with God and man, that it will never know itself as being otherwise than of the nature of the Eternal Goodness." [3]

4. In regard to Foreign Missions Bushnell felt that too much dependence was placed on organization, money, property, and the number of converts. He argued that both in the evangelistic campaign and in the missionary enterprise the method was that of organization, overpersuasion, force, conquest, and that the true growth and increase came through what he called "the outpopulating power of Christianity." That this position has triumphed is more than evidenced by the whole weight of the Laymen's Missionary

---

[1] *Religious Education*, vol. V, April 1910—February 1911, p. 102.

[2] Section 5, ps. 121-122.

[3] Archibald Warren Seymour, Horace Bushnell. Hartford, E. V. Mitchell. 1930. ps. 149-150.

Report. [1]   A very few sentences are quoted as illustrative of the whole.

"It is clearly not the duty of the Christian missionary to attack the non-Christian systems of religion. Nor is it his primary duty to denounce the errors and abuses he may see in them: it is his primary duty to present in positive form his conception of the true way of life and let it speak for itself." (p. 40).

"The Christian will therefore regard himself as a co-worker with the forces which are making for righteousness within every religious system. If he can in any way aid or encourage these forces, he will regard it a part of his Christian service to spend thought and energy in this way." (p. 66).

"Some of us found a young teacher in one of our larger oriental universities of whom we were told that every student who came into his classes was changed by the experience. There was no need for his students to have special chapel exercises for religion. He did not *urge* religion: he diffused Christianity." (p. 72).

The report believes in "evangelizing by living and by human service." The whole point is summed up almost in Bushnell's own phrase. "The Christian way of life and its spirit is capable of transmitting itself by quiet personal contact and by contagion: there are circumstances in which this is the most perfect mode of speech." The paragraph continues, "If the actual tasks of life can be shared with the people of a community, whatever power there is in the Christianity of the worker will be revealed in operation; and will do its part in transforming the spirit of in-

---

[1] *Re-Thinking Missions*, A Laymen's Inquiry after One Hundred Years. Harper and Brothers, New York, 1932.

dividual lives who perceive it. This also is evangelization, not by word but by deed." (p. 65).

The idea is expressed by William James in an address at Stanford University in his own graphic style: "Like a contagious disease, almost, spiritual life passes from man to man by contact . . . " Therefore, his advice to the University is "Above all things offer the opportunity of higher personal contacts."

Tennyson wrote

"Our echoes roll from soul to soul,
   And grow for ever and for ever."

There is no doubt that Bushnell foreshadowed in a wonderful way the position of present day liberals in regard to missions. The emphasis is on ministering to people and helping them to develop their own indigenous life and civilization in the spirit of the Master.

5.   Progressive Education. The founding of the Progressive Education Association made explicit what had long been implicit. There was a great gulf between the theories and practices of education as exemplified in the work of institutions and individuals. The demarcation is as real in church schools as in state schools. It is the fight between inculcating and transmitting knowledge on the one hand and nurturing and developing persons on the other.

In recent years substantial advances have been made. Public school educators have done yeoman service. There is space to mention but a very few here. Collings as early as 1923 after some years of practical work published *An Experiment with A Project Curriculum.* [1] Dr. John Dewey in his many books and pioneer work has laid a philosophi-

---

[1] The Macmillan Co., New York, 1923.

cal and experimental foundation. W. H. Kilpatrick contributed to method.[1] Innumerable experimenters in schools
have demonstrated pragmatically that the theory is sound.

In regard to the church school Erwin L. Shaver made
a contribution in emphasizing the project principle.[2] W. C.
Bower has written important books on the curriculum[3] and
on the place of experience in religious education.[4] Others
have demonstrated the theory in practice as for example
Sweet and Fahs[5] and Danielson and Perkins.[6] The principles and techniques of teaching have been stated in such
books as *The Child-Centered School* and *The New Leaven*
referred to on page 133; A. G. Melvin's *The Technique of
Progressive Teaching*[7]; Daniel J. Fleming's *Helping People
Grow*[8]; Hughes Mearns' *Creative Youth*[9] and *Creative
Power*[10]; Hartshorne and Lotz's *Case Studies of Present-
day Religious Teaching*[11]; and A. J. Wm. Myers' *Teaching
Religion Creatively.*[12]

This whole movement is in the spirit of the principles
expounded with so much eloquence and power by Horace
Bushnell.

[1] *Foundations of Method,* The Macmillan Co., New York, 1925.

[2] *The Project Principle in Religious Education,* University of Chicago Press, Chicago, 1924.

[3] *The Curriculum of Religious Education,* Chas. Scribner's Sons,
New York, 1925.

[4] *Character Through Creative Experience,* University of Chicago
Press, Chicago, 1930.

[5] *Exploring Religion with Eight Year Olds,* Henry Holt & Co., New
York, 1930.

[6] *Teaching Without Textbooks,* Pilgrim Press, Boston, 1930.

[7] John Day Co., New York, 1932.

[8] Association Press, New York, 1931.

[9] Doubleday, Page & Co., Garden City, N. Y., 1925.

[10] Doubleday, Doran & Co., Garden City, N. Y., 1929.

[11] Yale University Press, New Haven, 1932 and 1933.

[12] Fleming H. Revell Co., New York, 1932.

So much, then, for a brief consideration of Bushnell in relation to five great movements or organizations. Now the aim will be to take a few of Bushnell's chief tenets or theses from the quotations in the last chapter and see what place they have in religious education. These may be considered under six heads. As soon as they are formulated there is embarrassment at two points. In the first place the positions are no sooner stated than their truth and secure position today seem almost self-evident; and second, because the number of liberal educators is so great it is as impossible as it is unnecessary to refer to all of them. It is extraordinary that there should be such correspondence between liberal educators today and a writer whose book was published nearly one hundred years ago. The six positions will be considered in turn and reference made under each to a few modern leaders in religious education.

1. "There is then some kind of a nurture which is of the Lord. . . . The child should grow up a Christian, and never know himself as being otherwise." [1]

In these most striking sentences Bushnell attacked the whole intrenched doctrine of total depravity and was an outstanding champion of the great Charter of childhood laid down as fundamental by Jesus the Christ. "Let the children come to me, do not stop them: The Realm of God belongs to such as these." (Mk. 10:14—Moffatt's translation). The doctrine of total depravity is no longer a question among liberal educators.

But neither did he fall into the opposite error of believing every child to be totally angelic. He admitted what

---

[1] As expanded in the 1861 edition of *Christian Nurture*. See footnote 1 Chapter IV, p. 39.

he called "the natural pravity of man." [1] The dictionary makes pravity and depravity practically synonymous. But what he was feeling after seems clear enough. The child is neither totally depraved nor totally good. He has tendencies which may lead to good or bad living. If this is what Bushnell meant there is no position on which there is greater unanimity today.

That there is a nurture of the Lord is recognized by all Christians everywhere. The Jews always greatly emphasized this conviction. From very early days they insisted on the most careful religious training of the children in the home and at feasts and celebrations. The remarkable words of Deuteronomy, "And these words, which I command thee this day, shall be in thine heart: And thou shalt teach them diligently unto thy children, and shalt talk of them when thou sittest in thine house, and when thou walkest by the way, and when thou liest down, and when thou risest up" (6:6-7) have been a clarion call through the centuries.

This same aspect is magnified in the New Testament though, for various reasons, Paul's spectacular conversion has overshadowed it. All the disciples gained whatever insight they had by the quiet processes of education and contact with the great teacher. The major emphasis of the early church is expressed for all time in Second Timothy when the writer called "to remembrance the unfeigned faith" that characterized the young man and which he says "dwelt first in thy grandmother Lois, and thy mother Eunice." (1:5).

---

[1] *Views of Christian Nurture and of Subjects Adjacent Thereto*, p. 15.

The experience of the Moravian Church, which Bushnell cited, is well known. Through Christian education that church has maintained itself and produced an inspiring Christian experience. Many of its members would say with Count Zinzendorf that they never knew a time when they were not conscious of God and did not love Him. This, though it may not always be secured, is the high aim of educational evangelism. [1]

But in attempting to get a glimpse at what was the attitude to children one hundred years ago, in contradistinction to Bushnell's thesis, it is only fair to go to a friend of children and to one who wrote especially for them. No better friend can be found than the Rev. James Janeway, who published a little book entitled *A Token for Children; being an exact account of The Conversion, Holy Lives, and Joyful Deaths of Several Young Children*. The dedication is "To all Parents, Schoolmasters, and Schoolmistresses, or any that are concerned in the education of children." The prefatory note ends with these words: "That the young generation may be far more excellent than this, is the prayer of one that dearly loves little children." In it he says further: "I knew a child that was converted by this sentence from a godly school-mistress in the country— *Every mother's child of you are by nature children of wrath*. Put your children upon learning their catechism, and the scriptures, and getting to pray and weep by themselves after *Christ;* take heed of their company; take heed of pardoning a lie. . . . Let them read this book over a hundred times, and observe how they are *affected,* and ask them

---

[1] Myers, A. J. Wm. *Educational Evangelism,* National Sunday School Union, London, 1925.

what they think of those children, and whether they would
not be such; and follow what you do with earnest cries to
God, and be in travail to see Christ formed in their souls. [1]

In the "Preface: containing Directions to Children" he
says: "But tell me, my dear children and tell me truly, . . .
Did you ever see your miserable state by nature? Did you
ever get by yourselves and weep for sin, and pray for grace
and pardon? . . . Come, tell me truly, my dear child, for I
would fain do what I possibly can, to keep thee from falling
into everlasting fire. . . . And are you willing to go to hell
to be burned with the devil and his angels? . . . O! hell is
a terrible place; that is worse a thousand times than whip-
ping. God's anger is worse than your father's anger; and
are you willing to anger God? O child, this is most certainly true, that all that be wicked, and die so, must be
turned into hell; and if any be once there, there is no
coming out again. . . . Would you not do any thing in the
world, rather than be thrown into hell fire? Would you
not do any thing in the world to get Christ, grace and
glory? . . . How do you know but that you may be the next
child that may die? And where are you then if you be not
God's child?" (ps. 9-13). The concluding prayer of the
preface reads: "And that you may be your parents' joy,
your country's honor, and live in God's fear, and die in his
love, is the prayer of your dear friend, J. Janeway." (p. 18).

The book is comprised of thirteen chapters, each being
the description of a different child's experience,—and all of
them died young! The best way to get a picture of the
contents and of the conception of religious education involved is to read the captions of the chapters. [2]

---

[1] Robert Carter & Bros., New York, 1852. ps. 5-8.
[2] See Appendix p. 149.

A few sentences from Example II, about a child *between two and three years of age,* will indicate the teaching of the whole book:

"A certain little child, when he could not speak plain, would be crying after God, and was greatly desirous to be taught good things. . . . He was much delighted to hear the word of God, either read or preached. He loved to go to school, that he might learn something of God. . . . He quickly learned to read the Scriptures, and would, with great reverence and tenderness, read till tears and sobs were ready to hinder him. When he was at secret prayer, he would weep bitterly. . . . He was very fearful of wicked company, and would often beg of God to keep him from it. . . . He abhorred lying with his soul. When other children were playing, he would many a time and oft be praying. . . . That the same weak body that was buried in the churchyard, should be raised again, he thought very strange; but with admiration yielded that nothing was impossible to God; and that very day he was taken sick unto death. . . . He was asked. . . . Whether he were willing to die? He answered, Now I am willing, for I shall go to Christ. . . . He still grew weaker and weaker, but carried it with a great deal of sweetness and patience, waiting for his change, and at last did cheerfully commit his spirit unto the Lord; calling upon his name, and saying, Lord Jesus, Lord Jesus;—in whose bosom he sweetly slept, dying, as I remember, when he was about six years old." [1]

This makes sad reading. Children were considered totally depraved and lost. If saved, it was by miracle, and, even for children two and three years of age, only through the conversion experience. The appeal was based largely on the fear of death and hell. Passing from such a conception to the one generally held by religious educators today

---

[1] *A Token for Children,* ps. 36-43.

is like going from a dungeon out into the warmth and sunlight of a June day.

The Reverend Edward P. Hammond was a children's evangelist. In his book *The Conversion of Children*[1] he quotes several pages from Bushnell on a child growing up naturally in the Christian way, citing the Moravians, but the book is full of pathetic examples of young children being filled with a sense of sin and being converted. So people in those days as in the present, sometimes used labels of a new conception without grasping its spirit or understanding its significance.

Other churches have never had the idea of total depravity. George Parkins Atwater in his little book, *The Episcopal Church*[2] says: "Now the Episcopal Church has a very different attitude toward the children. It has the household idea. . . . The Church admits even babes into membership in the Household of faith." (ps. 51-52).

Because of G. Campbell Morgan's eminence as a preacher, acceptable even to very conservative groups, his concurrence with Bushnell's ideas will indicate something of the trend since his day. In an address on "The Claim of the Child" at the World's Sunday School Convention in Rome in 1907, Dr. Campbell Morgan pleads for better religious care of children. He says: "You would never have had a corrupt church and a false theology if in the midst of the church and in the midst of the schools of the church you had kept a little child, that men may understand the kingdom as it is, not as it is to be.

" . . . I would be sorry to base a theology on a single text, but I believe that the true method of dealing with the

---

[1] Funk & Wagnalls Co., New York, 1882.
[2] Morehouse Publishing Co., Milwaukee, 1917.

children is to tell them they belong to Christ from earliest childhood. I am not positive that every child needs conversion. . . . I don't know the day of my conversion. My brother, I do not undervalue your experience if you have such an hour, only don't let your volcanic method interfere with the gentler method." [1]

Studies in more recent years confirm Bushnell's position. Edwin D. Starbuck in his *Psychology of Religion* [2] and George A. Coe in *The Spiritual Life* [3] were forerunners of this new day. Almost every extensive survey made has shown that the vast majority of all church members have come through the natural processes of growth.

That religion is a natural phase of human life is claimed by countless writers. Rudolph M. Binder expresses it in the title of his book, *Religion as Man's Completion* [4] and substantiates his position in well founded argument. The testimony from primitive culture and foreign fields blot out the last vestiges of doubt. William C. Willoughby in his great book on *The Soul of the Bantu* shows how this splendid people have long known and sought after the living God. After many years in Africa where he lived in intimate contact with primitive peoples this able scholar sets down as his considered judgment "that the law of the upward urge (the attractive force of the Divine) is as universal in its application to humanity as the law of gravitation." [5]

---

[1] *Sunday Schools the World Around*. The official report of the World's Fifth Sunday-School Convention, in Rome, May 18-23, 1907. The World's Sunday-School Executive Committee, Philadelphia, 1907. ps. 65-69.

[2] Walter Scott, London, 1899.

[3] Fleming H. Revell Co., New York, 1909.

[4] Harper & Brothers, New York, 1927.

[5] Doubleday, Doran & Co., New York, 1928. p. vii.

W. B. Selbie in *The Psychology of Religion*[1] sums up
the attitude of most investigators in these words: "The
study of comparative religion and of the psychology of religion has made it more than ever evident that religion is
something natural to man, and is not imposed upon him
by an extraneous authority, art, or device. It belongs to
the very constitution of his nature. . . . Man is made that
way and can do no other if he is to fulfil his proper bent."
(p. 2). "He cannot help being religious, and the whole vast
and terrifying business which we call religion is rooted in
a nature which works in this way and can do no other."
(p. 31). " . . . Hence we cannot exaggerate the importance
of sound religious nurture. It is the prime condition of a
healthy development of our spiritual powers, and will do
more than perhaps anything else to secure a happy issue
from the spiritual an intellectual turmoil and tremors of
the adolescent period of our lives." (p. 185).

The authors of *The Psychology of Childhood*[2] say:
"The main thing for us as students of child psychology to
bear in mind is that children have a religious nature. To
ignore it is to deprive them of some of their inheritance,—
after all, the most important part." (ps. 235-236).

Since the Great War the question has often been asked
as to the future of the Church. Durant Drake in his book
Shall We Stand By The Church?[3] of which the subtitle is
A Dispassionate Inquiry says: "Education, then, the Christion education of youth, to a degree not yet attempted, is
our great need, if the new age is to increase or even to re-

---

[1] The Clarendon Press, Oxford, 1924.

[2] Norsworthy, Naomi and Whitley, Mary T., The Macmillan Co.,
New York, 1921.

[3] The Macmillan Co., New York, 1920.

tain, the spiritual heritage of the past. . . . We have learned that salvation comes normally through education; that must be our main reliance. Fortunately, in no field has there been more progress in the past decade." (ps. 113-114).

George Albert Coe's *Education in Religion and Morals* [1] rests on this conception of religious nurture. In A *Social Theory of Religious Education* [2] he quotes Bushnell's famous phrase with approval "That the child is to grow up a Christian, and never know himself as being otherwise" as does Myers in *What is Religious Education?* [3] The whole of Part III in Coe's book is an exposition of the naturalness of the religious life. Such books as Hugh Hartshorne's *Childhood and Character,* [4] Elizabeth Harrison's *A Study of Child Nature* [5] and many others are based on the same fundamental thesis.

The books of Patterson Du Bois [6] are moving expositions of this point of view and Mrs. Frances M. Morton's *First Steps in Religious Education,* [7] Mrs. Margaret Steven Moore's *Problems of a Little Child,* [8] H. W. Fox's *The Child's Approach to Religion,* [9] and T. Grigg-Smith's *The Child's Knowledge of God* [10] are eloquent pleas for the religious life of childhood. Mrs. Edith Mumford's *The Dawn*

---

[1] Fleming H. Revell Co., New York, 1909.

[2] Charles Scribner's Sons, New York, 1919.

[3] National Sunday School Union, London, 1925.

[4] Pilgrim Press, Boston, 1919.

[5] The Chicago Kindergarten College, Chicago, 42nd edition, 1911.

[6] *The Culture of Justice,* Dodd, Mead & Co., New York, 1907. *Fireside Child-study,* Dodd, Mead & Co., New York, 1913.

[7] Cokesbury Press, Nashville, Tenn.

[8] Pilgrim Press, Boston, 1928.

[9] Richard R. Smith, Inc., New York, 1930.

[10] Macmillan & Co., London, 1920.

of Religion in the Mind of a Child[1] is a classic on this subject.

A clear indication of the vast swing away from the conversion campaign to religious nurture is revealed in the statement of Dr. Cornelius H. Patton who, speaking of the admission of candidates to the ministry, said: "We have come almost to expect that candidates to-day will say, 'I do not know when I became a Christian.' The contrast of these figures with those for the first twenty years of the Board is instructive. . . . These figures, limited as they are plainly indicate that the nurture idea of the Christian life is gaining ground steadily in our midst."[2]

2. "Something like a law of organic connection" subsists between parent and child.

Bushnell's point here is substantiated by all modern students of education and sociology, though they would not state the case in the same words. Bushnell saw that the young person is conditioned by the family into which he is born, as definitely as if there were an organic bodily connection such as existed before birth. He saw clearly the fallacy in New England theology of treating each person as if he were an individual, distinct and separate from all others. It is essential for educators to consider the person in his total situation and associations. However stated, no position is more strongly held today.

Social heredity is perhaps the term which best expresses the thought Bushnell had in mind. Sociology is very strong on this point. Education has adopted its find-

---

[1] Longmans, Green & Co., New York, 1915.
[2] Proceedings of the Third Annual Convention of the Religious Education Association, Boston, Feb. 12-16, 1905. p. 165.

ings. W. F. Lofthouse's important work *Ethics and the Family* [1] makes a great deal of this position. "Whether the family ties are close-knit or loose, the family forms the immediate 'universe' of the majority of human beings. It is the source and medium, to the individual, of countless pleasures, pains, inconveniences, advantages, hopes, views, fears. . . . It will often decide a man's whole attitude to his life and his work, his country, and even to his morals and religion." (p. 6).

Progressive or creative education emphasises the same factor. Examples are found in Stanwood Cobb's *The New Leaven* [2] and Harold Rugg and Ann Shumaker's *The Child-Centered School.* [3] Myers in *Teaching Religion Creatively* [4] makes it a major point that the pupil must be considered in his total situation.

Sociologists long ago stressed greatly the importance of the primary groups. Henry F. Cope's book *Religious Education in the Family* [5] made a distinct contribution to religious thinking along this line. Ernest R. Groves [6] and many other writers insist on the fundamental importance of its continuous and pervasive influence on the children. James B. Pratt in *The Religious Consciousness* [7] has a striking chapter on the religion of childhood which substantiates both the points so far considered. It would seem from

---

[1] Hodder and Stoughton, London.

[2] John Day Co., New York, 1928.

[3] World Book Co., Yonkers-on-Hudson, New York, 1928.

[4] Fleming H. Revell Co., New York, 1932.

[5] University of Chicago Press, Chicago, 1915.

[6] *American Marriage and Family Relationships*, H. Holt & Co., New York, 1928. *Social Problems of the Family*, J. B. Lippincott & Co., Philadelphia, 1927.

[7] The Macmillan Co., New York, 1921.

these and an almost unlimited number of other writers that the essential conception for which Bushnell stood is a commonplace in religious thought today.

3.   The home should be characterized by camaraderie and love with the type of control and freedom gained in this way alone.   But in the majority of cases in that day authority was backed up by a liberal application of the rod. The public school used very freely the birch, the cat, and other instruments of torture.   Indeed, an old symbol of the teacher was the hornbook and a bunch of birch rods.

Bushnell not only preached these doctrines of camaraderie and of Christian nurture but he and his wife practiced them.   References in his biographies and intimate sketches of friends picture a lovely home life.   It is also best revealed in his letters, two of which are included in the Appendix. [1]

In the century since Bushnell, even such a conservative institution as the public school has surrendered, bit by bit, the use of corporal punishment until in most enlightened countries it is practically prohibited.

The home has made equally great progress.   One of the most delightful things about present conditions, however dark they may be, is the camaraderie between parents and children in the more intelligent homes.   The desirability of such an atmosphere is so recognized that it needs no argument.   George Walter Fiske in *The Changing Family* [2] has a chapter on home tyranny, anarchy, and democracy which may be taken as broadly representative of present attitudes.

---

[1] Ps. 180-183.

[2] Harper & Bros., New York, 1928. ps. 188-200.

In religious education this warm friendliness between teacher and class has long been emphasized. The Character Education Inquiry [1] has shown that this is one of the most important character forming influences in education.

From intensive study of adolescents Earl S. Rudisill in *Intimate Problems of Youth* [2] says: "In addition to religious instruction the system of religious training will have to include a serious effort to meet the adolescent on the level of his intimate problems." (p. 49). And he adds that one of the most important influences in life is proper "adjustment within one's home." (p. 59). The whole weight of social psychology and remedial treatment supports Bushnell in a new way in his emphasis on the primary importance of the spirit and atmosphere of the home.

Even in Bushnell's own day as evidenced by the reviews already quoted there was almost unanimous support on the part of liberals and conservatives, friends and enemies, of his pleas for homes being expressly religious. Every religious educator of today stands strongly for this as one of the greatest needs of the hour.

4.   Growth not Conquest is the true means of extending the Kingdom.

One hundred years ago the evangelistic campaign and the foreign missionary movement had tremendous vogue. The former as previous chapters have shown was in many minds almost synonymous with church life. Bushnell became more and more convinced that the evangelistic campaign was a delusion. He maintained this position courageously and at great personal cost.

---

[1] Hartshorne and May, *Studies in Deceit*, The Macmillan Co., New York, 1928.

[2] The Macmillan Co., New York, 1929.

The attitude of the Christian church to these campaigns is no longer a question. Though they raged like forest fires under such leaders as Moody and Sankey, Chapman and Alexander, Torrey, Billy Sunday, and Aimee Semple McPherson, they are not now sought after [1] by liberal churches. The early investigations of Coe and Starbuck already referred to; William James's enlightening *Varieties of Religious Experience;* [2] Frederick M. Davenport's rather devastating *Primitive Traits in Religious Revivals;* [3] James B. Pratt's incisive analysis of "Crowd Psychology and Revival"; [4] to mention only a few writers, exposed the fallacious side of the evangelistic campaign. Charles C. McKinley's book on "Educational Evangelism," [5] Myers' book of the same title, [6] "Hocking's "Evangelism" [7] and many others emphasize the constructive evangelism inherent in religious education.

But more important still was the growing conviction of the church based on its history that the educational way and the influence of personal friendship are the true methods of developing Christian character.

Washington Gladden is one of the most representative preachers of the last generation. He quotes [8] at length from Bushnell, supporting strongly the theory that education and

---

[1] Page 132.

[2] Longmans, Green & Co., New York, 1903.

[3] The Macmillan Co., New York, 1905.

[4] *The Religious Consciousness*, Chapter IX. See footnote 7, p. 133.

[5] Pilgrim Press, Boston, 1905.

[6] See footnote 1, p. 125. Chapter VI.

[7] Hocking, William Ernest. Privately printed, 1935. 44 ps.

[8] *The Christian Pastor and The Working Church* in the International Theological Library, T. & T. Clark, Edinburgh, 1898. Chapter XVII Revivals & Revivalism. ps. 379-400.

family religion is the best way to promote the Kingdom of God. His words may well be pondered and acted upon by the church today. "His (Bushnell's) argument is that if the Church simply *holds its own*, its growth will be rapid, even phenomenal. If the children of Christian families are kept in the Church and trained for efficient service, if the organic life of the Church is as vigorous as it ought to be, its own law of natural increase will speedily put it in possession of the world." (p. 387).

John G. McKenzie could not more fully confirm Bushnell's position if he were replying directly to the question as to what modern psychology had to say about it. He writes "It is perhaps unfortunate that the term *conversion,* as generally used, has been almost exclusively applied to those who can name a day and hour when they turned from sin to Christ. . . . Indeed, what is the whole aim of our teaching if not to prevent the necessity of any such break in coming to a conscious recognition of the Lordship of Christ? They ought to grow into the kingdom." [1]

And he continues "Have the piety of the parents, the faithfulness of teachers anything to do with the number of Christian workers? Everything. It is they who help the child to acquire that religious sentiment to which the appeal that leads to decision or conversion is made, and without it no decision or conversion is possible." (p. 103).

And finally, not to extend the references indefinitely, the Wiemans' very significant work [2] strikingly substantiates all four points emphasized above. Of course, the au-

---

[1] *Modern Psychology and the Achievement of Christian Personality,* the National Sunday School Union, London. p. 97.

[2] Wieman, Henry Nelson and Wieman, Regina Westcott, *Normative Psychology of Religion.* Thomas Y. Crowell Co., New York, 1935. p. 564.

thors go far beyond what Bushnell wrote but several of the main ideas were there, more than in germ, in his little book.

5. Teaching suited to the age of the pupil.

In 1847 the Sunday School taught the Catechism, creeds and Scripture by memory. It was not until 1872 that Uniform Lessons were issued. In these, as is well known, the same Bible passage was assigned to every class in the Sunday School. Bushnell, a whole generation earlier, advanced the position that the material should be suited to the pupil.

This links him up with all those who in the following years fought for this principle.[1] It is not possible even to mention any large proportion of all those who worked for graded worship and graded studies. Several pages of names would make an impressive array but would be invidious, omitting many who should be included. The words of the writer of Hebrews may well be quoted "And what shall I more say? for the time would fail me" even to recount any considerable number of them.

6. Experience rather than doctrine is the basis of teaching.

This emphasis has come into the focus of attention in the last few years as a major consideration in the development of courses of study or as the term is commonly used, enterprises or units of work. No one can imagine that Bushnell had the same thing in mind, but there is no doubt that he had a glimpse of the fundamental germinal idea.

And this is not so astonishing. Most wise parents have the same basic notion though they may be too inarticulate

---

[1] Myers, A. J. Wm. *The Old Testament in the Sunday School.* Teachers College, New York, 1912. p. 141.

to express it. Their aim has always been to help their children as they would say, to *be* good. It is difficult to improve on that expression. It is not a question of knowing facts or dogmas so much as it is a question of the spiritual life.

In Bushnell's time Sunday school study consisted largely in memorizing creeds and Scripture verses. This too great dependence on teaching verbal statements has gradually given way to leading and guiding people in their everyday experience and in meeting the social issues of life and so in helping them to know God. It is the personal experience of God which is formative. "Parents," said Bushnell, "should rather seek to teach a feeling than a doctrine, to bathe the child in their own feeling of love to God, and dependence on him." (p. 36). "The virtue of the truly good and sanctified life" is magnified for it is "so much easier to be violent than to be holy." (p. 41.) "Religion never penetrates life till it becomes domestic." (p. 45). These are as true for the church as for the home.

It is natural that Bushnell should feel this strongly. He was no narrow ecclesiastic. He was one of those people who have such a warmth and depth of soul that they almost instinctively lay hold of human values in spite of all conventions that entrap lesser minds. He knew that the supreme value was the human soul and its own experiencing of God and its growth in human fellowship.

It is but a truism to assert that one important trend in education, religious and secular, is precisely in this direction. Practically every forward-looking teacher and writer emphasizes it and this tendency certainly follows the trail blazed by Horace Bushnell in his inspiring and prophetic treatise.

There are two other points, perhaps not brought out so much in his writings but emphasized at every turn in his life, which should not be passed by, namely the emphasis on creating a new society—a new civilization where one lives, not merely talking about it, and the necessity for the leader to have many and broad interests. No religious leader can do his best work if he is confined within his own little system and round of duties. He ought to have a wealth of interests and many contacts. These two points are supremely exemplified in Bushnell.

The Kingdom of God is not a matter of sentimental words. It implies the painful struggle to help society carry on business and politics in the spirit of Jesus; and peoples and nations of all faiths and creeds to live and work together like children of the Father. The religious leader must be forward in every good work that promotes the best welfare of mankind. He must be a good citizen. To Bushnell religion was coterminous with life and he fought with all his skill and energy and at great personal cost for social reforms in his own city and in the world.

The breadth of his interests and the range of his abilities are referred to by any number of writers. The following excerpts are taken from an article by Walter Allen in *The Atlantic Monthly* of March, 1900.[1] "His published sermons live. . . . And literature will be apt to treasure some of these sermons, with many of his essays and addresses, as choice trophies of achievement in the art of English expression.

"During the whole term of his pastorate, and until the end of his life, he was the public-spirited citizen, actively

---

[1] Vol. LXXXV, No. DIX. Article, "Horace Bushnell".

promoting the prosperity of his city and state, and giving to the affairs of the nation earnest attention. He kept abreast of the current social and political movements of a history-making epoch, and when occasion served gave valorous help to the righteous side. His first published sermon (1835) was entitled The Crisis of the Church. In it he arraigned slavery as an impending peril. . . .

"From that time onward to the outbreak of the slaveholders' rebellion, and through the agony of the war . . . he kept his influence steadily useful to the party of freedom. . . .

"In an oration in 1865 he proposed an amendment to the Constitution, providing that 'the basis of representation in Congress shall be the number, in all the states alike, of the free male voters therein.' . . .

"In 1840, sixty years ago, he uttered a denunciation of the immoral spoils system of party government that has not been bettered in the long interval since. . . .

"He was an earnest ally of public education in its lower and its higher realms. At a time when the Hartford schools were in a low state he was active in stimulating public opinion to lift them up, and his effort produced great and permanent effects. . . . During a year spent in California, sick man that he was, he devoted himself with ardor to forwarding the project of a university, giving impulse to a nascent public sentiment which has blossomed gloriously. This is only one of the ways in which he exerted a beneficent influence in moulding the young commonwealth, whose promise he measured with a statesman's prescience.

"Rev. J. H. Twichell, of Hartford, has said, 'Bushnell lies back of all that is best in the city.' Another says,

'Hartford is largely what he has made it.' In a time of stagnation and discouragement, he roused the citizenship to confidence and fresh endeavor by a notable sermon entitled Prosperity a Duty. When the community had been induced to substantial agreement to build the new State House on an unfit site, he went into a public meeting and made an address which changed the aspect of the matter so decisively that the scheme was no longer tolerable. By a labor begun almost alone, and continued through years as tactfully as persistently, he prevailed in reclaiming an unsightly and nauseous region in the heart of the city and transforming it into a park, which, while he lay dying, was by vote of the city government named Bushnell Park. All these things, and many more that cannot be enumerated, were accomplished by sheer ability to impress his better judgment on the conviction of men of affairs. . . .

"All in all, he must be accounted a man of noble stature, whose work promoted that conception of God as love which

'Would change the hue of intermediate things
And make one thing of all theology.' " (ps. 421-425).

The Rev. N. H. Egleston is quoted [1] as saying of Bushnell: "What interest of Hartford is not to-day indebted to him? Do we speak of schools? . . . The city is indebted to no one more than to Dr. Bushnell for the new impulse which lifted its schools to their present grade of excellence. Do we speak of taste and culture? Who has been a nobler example and illustration of both, or who has by his just criticism and various instructions so aided in their development? If we turn to the business interests of the city, who

---

[1] *The New England Magazine*, January, 1900, Vol. XXI, No. 5. Warren F. Kellogg, Boston, Mass. ps. 639-640.

of its older residents does not remember how, years ago, at a time when the impression had become prevalent that Hartford had reached its growth, that it was declining, while other cities were outstripping it, Dr. Bushnell lifted himself up in that crisis and asserted not only the ability but the duty of the city to prosper, and how he woke the city to new life, and gave an impulse which has been felt to this day? Hartford feels him to-day everywhere. It may be doubted whether another instance in our own history is to be found of a man impressing himself in so many ways and with such force upon a place of such size and importance as this. Hartford is largely what he has made it."

The editor of this same magazine [1] concludes the article in which some indication is given of his many varied interests with the sentence: "True citizen of the little Litchfield county town, true citizen of Connecticut, true citizen of America, true citizen of the world, true citizen, in each and all of these earthly circles, of the divine commonwealth, the kingdom of God,—such was Horace Bushnell."

And in these no mention is made of his skill as an engineer in laying out roads, suggesting the best route for the railway to California, selecting the university site there, pointing out a better location for San Francisco; his mechanical skill as exhibited in building in stone; his athletic prowess; interest in nature, in fishing, in hiking; his love of music and founding of the Yale Beethoven Society; his genius as a writer and creator of literature; his powers of oratory and the brilliance and depth of his thought.

Progressive religious educators to-day feel they must be good citizens interested in the promotion of culture and

---

[1] Edwin D. Mead—"Editor's Table." p. 644.

of all social improvement and must also have a width of interests beyond the scope of their own particular and immediate work.

Summing up Bushnell's influences after well nigh a century has passed in which more profound and rapid changes have occurred than in any other period in history, it is surely remarkable that the main ideas and even the phrases and sentences of a speaker and author should still be current among the progressive leaders of the day. This is not because progress has not moved beyond Bushnell's dreams, but it is because of the fact that he grasped certain great fundamental ideas with the sureness and keenness of insight of the true prophet. It may be well, in conclusion, to set down a few of these, the mere statement of which is almost sufficient to secure general assent to their validity.

"That a child is to grow up a Christian, and never know himself as being otherwise" has been one of the most dynamic sentences in religious literature. The ideal embodied is the aim of all progressive religious education.

Growth, development, and words of similar meaning express a central thought of all education as over against indoctrination and revivalism.

The "outpopulating power of Christianity" is now recognized as the legitimate method in missions. Expansion by "conquest" is discredited. The aim of developing an indigenous, autonomous native church is quite generally accepted.

Bushnell's idea of education and religion was the emancipation of the personality. This is the keynote of all progressives in both fields today.

The tremendous importance of the first few years of a child's life in shaping his destiny is now being stressed by experts in child study. Bushnell's passages on this are strangely modern.

In the idea of the organic unity of the family, though not developed in detail and imperfect as stated, is embodied the well established conception of social heredity which, in its main positions no one thinks of questioning.

The emphasis placed on every day religion and practice in the home, at work and play, and on the friendliness, camaraderie, warmth, and glow of intimate groups as most potential factors in the development of good character is substantiated by the most recent scientific studies.

A characteristic of many religious people was their defence of the faith handed down and considered orthodox. But Bushnell had the scientific attitude, holding opinions tentatively in the sense that he was ever ready to change his position if new light warranted it. He was ever forward-looking, eagerly anticipating new truth.

Play was not in his day given the dignified place it now holds both in education and in life. His address on "Work and Play" is quite in keeping with the spirit of educators at the present time.

The passing away of the divisive elements in denominationalism is hailed as a triumph of the better spirit. "We find him in complete freedom from all sectarian trammels; adopting in genuine catholicity of spirit, wise teaching wherever he might find it," wrote the Rev. G. S. Drew, in *The Contemporary Review,* London.[1] This was the observation of a contemporary, not of one writing long afterwards.

---

[1] August, 1879, V. XXXV, ps. 815-831. Article, "An American Divine; Horace Bushnell, D.D."

Among Bushnell's writings after the publication of *Christian Nurture* the most remarkable contributions were his great works on *Nature and the Supernatural* and *God in Christ*—the main conceptions of both being in keeping with modern progressive thought.

Bushnell was ever a champion of the public school, but the public school at its best. Of course, his interest in higher education is well known, especially in connection with the University of California.

Religious educators are today stressing the fact that they must themselves have wider interests and must consider the total community and world situation in which their people find themselves. Here Bushnell led the way. He made his influence felt in municipal, state, and national affairs, in education and business, and in almost every aspect of the life of his time. He possessed that quality so much needed in religious educators—an unquenchable interest and faith in *people*.

Bushnell emphasized the authority of experience. The memorizing of words or accepting creeds is not a vitalizing force like knowing God. He held with the mystics in a sense that direct experience is a fact as basic as any other science. This, coupled with his revolt against the tyranny of formulated definitions, delivers from at least one form of literalism. With him as with educators today, religion is a growing, developing experience.

Perhaps one of his most creative ideas is that there must ever be a search after truth. The orthodoxy of the day tied up each bundle of doctrine in a neat and tidy definition. Against this he protested with all his might, arguing that words at best are symbols and that great conceptions can never be reduced to exact and precise formulae.

He even went so far as to hold that theologians did not know all that could be discovered about God! This search for a fuller conception of God is characteristic of "God's experimenters" of every age. In the continuous prosecution of this search lies the surest hope for the future.

In 1932 in Pilgrim Place, Claremont, California, one of the houses just built was called "Horace Bushnell House." At the dedication Professor George Albert Coe (who suggested the name) was one of the speakers. Always keenly penetrating in analysis, Dr. Coe said in part:

"Though he held to much in the way of theology that was to pass away, even holding it utterly essential, nevertheless he took his characteristic stand, made his characteristic emphasis and interpretations, at the *growing points,* not the dying points.

"His view of the organic relation of the individual mind to the group anticipated the social psychology of our day.

"His conception of education as growth put him in the line of the greatest of the educational reformers, though I have not discovered that he was acquainted with them."

Bushnell himself was growing, ever looking onward, anticipating the "yet greater things". No human mind can grasp all truth or compass any considerable proportion of it. It is a matter of emphasis and whether one stresses the living or dying matters mightily. This word of one creative mind about another is a fitting tribute which one cannot but feel Bushnell would like. "He stressed the *growing points,* not the dying points." Therein lies something of the secret of creative thought.

CHAPTER VII

THE JUDGMENT OF HISTORY

S EVERAL writers and speakers, especially during the controversy, rested their cases against Bushnell and his teaching by an appeal to the judgment of history. To history this and all other matters must go for final arbitrament. It is, of course, impossible to cite any great number of witnesses, but a fairly wide sampling is here submitted. From all the evidence. these verdicts are unescapable: 1) Bushnell was one of the prophetic souls who *saw* truth. He was not a laborious, systematic thinker but he had the gift of seeing and expressing living, growing elements of thought and experience; and 2) the genius of his life and his outlook both concerning nature, man and God, though imperfect in many particulars, anticipated much of the spirit of present-day religious education, and was wondrously modern in its expression. Many of the excerpts in Chapter V are as timely today as when they were first written. The issues he raised are vital; they have the quality of life. As the writer in *The New-England Religious Herald* of September 11, 1847, in his review of *Christian Nurture* said prophetically: "The fame of his 'Discourses' has gone over the whole country, and the spirit of inquiry, excited by them, has penetrated every sect. The questions started will not die of inanition; they must be *settled.* . . . Arguments, though they are as numerous as the particles of sand in the vessel, will not bury it." (p. 4).

It seems best to arrange the material in the order of
the date of publication rather than to attempt to classify it
topically. The aim is to discover something of the judgment of succeeding years on Bushnell's main ideas and
whether they are vital today.

Dr. Henry M. Goodwin dedicated his *Christ and Humanity* to Bushnell, "whose profound and sanctified genius
has made the world his debtor." And he argues, like Bushnell, for *"the essential unity of the divine and human"* in
which he finds the basis for hope in developing individual
and social life according to the ideals of Jesus. [1]

Dr. Bartol, a close personal friend, in a chapter on
"Bushnell the Theologian", said "But this supersubtle rea-
soner concerning the native corruption of the race, in his
discourses on 'Christian Nurture', struck at the doctrine of
total depravity the heaviest blow it has ever received." [2]
Dr. Bartol continues: "His elucidation and courageous re-
assertion of this so well-taken point after a long ecclesiastical dullness made the Church ring all its bells once more!
But at the touch of reproach and persecution he did not
waver or flinch. . . . The volume of sermons, which were
dissertations on the Church as being a nursery and not a
revival camp or rink, was the most valuable of his publications, for all parties in our New England Christendom
of thirty years ago. . . . The pages of Bushnell have a fresh
stimulus and generous nutriment still, as of communion
bread and wine." (p. 373).

---

[1] Buckham, John Wright. *Progressive Religious Thought In
America,* Boston and New York, Houghton Mifflin Co., The Riverside
Press, Cambridge, 1919. Introduction, p. 31, footnote.

[2] Bartol, Cyrus Augustus. *Principles and Portraits,* Boston, Rob-
erts Brothers, 1880. p. 372.

The appearance of his daughter's biography *Life and Letters of Horace Bushnell* [1] was the occasion for the leading magazines not only to review the book but to express themselves on Bushnell's work. To say that they took full advantage of this is an understatement. The extent of some of these reviews is so considerable that the number of pages is occasionally stated. What would a writer today think if leading magazines devoted from thirty to sixty pages to a commendatory review of his book!

The New Englander [2] review comprised sixty-three pages of enthusiastic appraisal of Bushnell. The writer's main points may be set forth briefly in these sentences: "The name of Horace Bushnell is one of the great names of modern theological literature, and one destined to become still greater and more widely honored as his quickening thought penetrates more deeply the thought and theology of the age." . . . He is "a great religious teacher and reformer, a true prophet and interpreter of the ways of God, one of the few raised up and inspired of God to enlarge the boundaries of truth". He likens him to Columbus, Copernicus, Newton, and Luther and continues "That this prophetic gift, the illumination of the Spirit to discern, and the power of utterance to declare divine truth, was vouchsafed to Horace Bushnell, if to any in modern times, no thoughtful and unprejudiced reader of this memoir will be disposed to question." (ps. 803-804). Of Bushnell's picture he wrote: "Such a countenance, so pure, and spiritual, and meditative, might have stood for the Apostle John

---

[1] Cheney, Mary Bushnell, Harper & Brothers, N. Y., 1880.

[2] Vol. XXXIX, ps. 803-827; and Vol. XL, ps. 1-39. (December 1880 and January 1881). The article is entitled "Horace Bushnell" and is by Rev. Mr. Goodwin, of Olivet, Michigan.

studying the Holy Scriptures." (p. 808). (See frontispiece).

Summing up with an estimate of Bushnell's "character and genius" he says: "If any one trait or quality was supreme in him, it was his intense love and devotion to *truth*. This was, in fact, the master principle of his character. . . . The first element or characteristic of his genius was the *purity* and *singleness* of his devotion to truth—loving it supremely for itself, and rejoicing in it as its own exceeding great reward.

"This intense love of truth and impatience of all shams and disguises and mere conventionalities, gave character . . . to his style of discourse and his words, whether written or spoken. These were as original as his thought. . . . He was impatient of the verbiage in which many writers drown or dilute their thoughts. He used only the most necessary and fitting words, and his written style is a marvel and model of condensed and vitalized language.

"Combined with this perfect honesty of vision and conviction, and with this transparency of motive and expression, was a total self-surrender to the truth, as worthy of absolute trust and obedience. [1] . . . *Conscientiousness,* or moral integrity in the pursuit of truth, was another characteristic. . . . Another central principle of his character and genius was *faith* (p. 34). . . . It is not perhaps too much to assert that the true greatness of Dr. Bushnell consisted, or at least culminated, in his *piety*. The one lesson which comes out in every page of his biography is the essential affinity between godliness and the very highest genius, as well as the noblest and grandest character." (p. 35).

---

[1] *The New Englander*, January, 1881. ps. 32-33.

"One marked feature of his piety was the freedom yet elevation of his converse with God. He found society in this converse, as the greatest poets have found society in Nature. . . . The order and quality of his mind was as rare as his piety was profound. This was preeminently *intuitional*, not logical or ratiocinative,—that order of intellect which is represented by Plato among the ancients, by St. John among the Apostles, and by Coleridge among the moderns." (ps. 36-37).

"Unlike most men of such a spiritual order of mind, he had a large *humanity*, and took a living practical interest in men and things. . . . There was hardly any form of manual work or mechanical skill with which he was not practically familiar. He might have been an architect, an engineer, or an inventor, if he had not been a theologian. . . . What his creative genius accomplished for the city of Hartford, in the beautiful park which is its noblest ornament, has already been told. One of the rewards of this labor, which afforded him the purest delight, was witnessing in his walks upon it during his invalid days, the enjoyment of the populace, who passed him without knowing their great benefactor. . . .

"What place he will hold hereafter in the pantheon of literature and theological thought it may be premature to attempt to say. But the conviction that remains after the closest acquaintance, and the most careful study of the man and his works, is that a grander intellect and a purer soul has not appeared on this earth since Milton left it." (ps. 38-39).

Prof. George P. Fisher, in his notice in *The International Review* [1] of Mrs. Cheney's biography, refers particu-

---

[1] January, 1881. Vol. X, No. 1. Article, "Horace Bushnell".

larly to his literary style and his many interests. "The extraordinary fascination of Dr. Bushnell's literary addresses," he says, "has been allowed by the most censorious of his theological critics. Depth of thought, liveliness of imagination, and brilliancy of diction are seldom mingled in a more effective union. His Phi Beta Kappa oration at Cambridge on 'Work and Play', which was written when he was in the heat of his theological conflict, had all the freshness of a mountain stream in the Adirondack forests, where he loved to wander. To our mind the finest illustration of his peculiar power as a literary artist is his discourse at the Litchfield centennial celebration in 1851, on 'The Age of Homespun'. No painting, or series of paintings, could more vividly picture the New England of the old time. Home and school and church, household life and village ways, as they existed in the author's boyhood, are reproduced with the skill of a Rembrandt. The veil is lifted with a reverent hand, yet with constant touches of delicate humor; and New England society, before the quiet old Puritan era had passed by, is delineated before the eyes of a new generation. . . .

"Dr. Bushnell was no unpractical recluse; he was no dreamy mystic. . . . On matters like housebuilding and church-building, farming, and the various handicrafts which call into exercise mechanical ingenuity, his judgments were those of a connoisseur. He invented a furnace. He taught the people of Hartford how to make a beautiful park out of an unsightly mud-flat, and they becomingly called the new creation by his name. A robust commonsense was a marked quality of his mind." (ps. 24-25).

Over and over again writers bear testimony to the influence of Bushnell's personality and the expansive power

of his ideas. C. C. Nott in *The Nation, August,* 1880 [1]
writes: "He did not command men; he did not lead them,
he did not even convince them. He established no sect; he
founded no school, he left no accepted system, and from a
doctrinal point of view he had no following. . . . Nevertheless, the influence of Dr. Bushnell has been a great
power, steadily making its own way, constantly, like water,
expanding and permeating. If other men have not adopted
his enlarged horizon, they have, in consequence of his teaching, enlarged their own. If his arguments did not storm
the intrenched camp of the 'schools', his influence gradually
levelled their fortifications and brought the defenders out
into a broader plain of theologic liberality."

The Rev. Amos S. Chesebrough, one of his intimate
friends, gives his own judgment and that of Dr. Bartol on
the importance of *Christian Nurture*. In an article in *The
Andover Review* of August, 1886, entitled "The Theological
Opinions of Horace Bushnell as Related to His Character
and Christian Experience" he wrote "What he (Bushnell)
had learned from his own experience, for example of the
real elements of power in the Christian household, was embodied in his matchless Discourses on Christian Nurture,
which I am inclined, with Dr. Bartol, to regard as 'his most
important contribution to the church'. Touching with a
master's hand the secret springs of plastic young life, these
sermons have a far-seeing, prophetic look towards that on
which the future progress and triumph of the church
mainly depend." [2] His moving words to parents urging

---

[1] Volume 31, August 19, 1880. New York, E. L. Godkin & Co. Article, "Dr. Bushnell". p. 137.

[2] A Religious and Theological Monthly. Vol. VI. July-December,
1886. Boston, Houghton Mifflin and Co. The Riverside Press, Cambridge.

that they live their Christianity in their everyday life in the home are as fresh and as appealing as when they were written and are commended to all who have the interests of Christian character at heart.

Remembering Tyler's appeal to history, the following from *The Library of the World's Best Literature, Ancient and Modern* [1] is interesting: "It is now generally acknowledged that he led the way into the new world of theological thought which has since opened so widely, and thereby rendered so great and enduring service to the Christian faith. . . . He was the first theologian in New England to admit fully into his thought the modern sense of Nature, as it is found in the literature of the early part of the century, and notably in Wordsworth and Coleridge. . . . The secret of this movement was a spiritual interpretation of nature. . . . The thing that the world is rapidly learning is that not only is the world God's but that God is in his world.

"At the bottom of all his work lies a profound sense of nature, of its meaning and force in the realm of the spirit. He did not deny a certain antithesis between nature and the supernatural, but he so defined the latter that the two could be embraced in the one category of nature when viewed as the ascertained order of God in creation. The supernatural is simply the realm of freedom, and it is as natural as the physical realm of necessity. Thus he not only got rid of the traditional antinomy between them, but led the way into that conception of the relation of God to his world which more and more is taking possession of modern thought. (ps. 2909-2910).

---

[1] Warner, Charles Dudley, editor. 30 volumes. Volume 5. New York, R. S. Peale and J. A. Hill, 1897.

"Perhaps his most influential book is the first, 'Christian Nurture'; while a treatise for the household, it was surcharged with theological opinions which proved to be revolutionary and epoch-making. 'The Vicarious Sacrifice' has most affected the pulpit. 'Nature and the Supernatural' the tenth chapter of which has become a classic, has done great service in driving out the extreme dualism that invested the subject of God's relation to creation. His ablest essay is the treatise on Language; the most literary is that on 'Work and Play'; the most penetrating in its insight is 'Our Gospel a Gift to the Imagination'; the most personal and characteristic is 'The Age of Homespun'. His best sermon is always the one last read; and they are perhaps his most representative work." (p. 2914).

Not only did Bushnell affect theology and education, but his influence on preaching was very great. Two outstanding ministers who have done much to make the pulpit a mighty power were Phillips Brooks and Washington Gladden. These are names to conjure with not only in church circles but in the world at large. Bushnell's influence on them may not be generally known.

The Christmas, 1899, number of *The New England Magazine* contains a long editorial on Bushnell. The author recalls that at a memorial service to Phillips Brooks, his successor, Dr. Donald, observed that Brooks' contribution was not "anything distinctly original" for his theology was "simply the theology of Bushnell." [1]

The editor continues: "This is substantially the truth; and it could be said of great numbers of the most thoughtful and influential men in the American pulpit to-day. In

---

[1] Volume XXXI, Editor's Table—Edwin D. Mead. Boston, Warren F. Kellogg.

the religious turmoil and confusion of a generation ago, Bushnell was a great light and a positive guide, mediating to many minds a rational theology and a noble and satisfying method. Washington Gladden undoubtedly spoke for hundreds when he recently wrote: 'I could not have remained in the ministry, an honest man, if it had not been for him. The time came, long before I saw him, when the legal or forensic theories of the Atonement were not true for me; if I had not found his 'God in Christ' and 'Christ in Theology', I must have stopped preaching. Dr. Bushnell gave me a moral theology, and helped me to believe in the justice of God. If I have had any gospel to preach during the last thirty-five years, it is because he led me into the light and joy of it.'

"Horace Bushnell was certainly the most original and influential theologian in New England in this last half of the nineteenth century save Theodore Parker alone. . . . (p. 505).

" 'Christian Nurture', 'The Vicarious Sacrifice', 'God in Christ', 'Christ and his Salvation',—each of these works bore in it a revolution for American religious thought and life. Epoch-making above all was the work on 'Nature and the Supernatural'. . . . The power of Bushnell was not so much in the new doctrines which he taught, although he was a prolific, radical and sweeping teacher of new doctrines, as in the new and inspiring spirit, the spirit of nature and of freedom, which he brought to every question.

"Professor George Adam Smith has said that Bushnell is the preacher's preacher, as Spenser is the poet's poet. His early sermon on 'Every Man's Life a Plan of God' has been spoken of by one enthusiast as 'one of the three greatest sermons ever preached.' (p. 506).

"If there be a prose counterpart to 'The Cotter's Saturday Night' and 'Snow Bound', it is 'The Age of Homespun'. . . . There is not in our New England literature any other work which shows with such true sympathy and understanding, such sturdiness and tenderness and insight, the character of the people of the Old New England country and the spirit which has created what is best and most enduring in New England and in the nation." (p. 509).

Dr. Munger in his biography is not given to overstatement. He calls attention to several aspects of Bushnell's genius. He says: "We cannot pass by 'Christian Nurture' as it appears in the later full edition without once more calling attention to it as an achievement in the world of New England theology. . . . The greatness of the book as an intellectual achievement has not had full recognition, chiefly because its theological surroundings have not been understood. It is not in its essence a discovery, for its main idea lies at the bottom of all the historic religions. . . . Biblical interpretation, psychology, and the closer study of life in all its departments are forcing theology to recognize the fact that Christian character is chiefly a matter of Christian nurture. [1]

". . . The dialectic habit with such men necessarily led to a hard and rigid use of language. Their strength lay in definition and logic, which were often used in such a way as to suggest a corral rather than a teaching." (p. 101). One of Bushnell's vital contributions was that he refused to conceive of the Spirit in mechanical terms as did some of the New England theologians. Munger quotes

---

[1] Munger, Theodore T. *Horace Bushnell: Preacher and Theologian.* Boston and New York, Houghton Mifflin & Co., 1899. ps. 95-97.

him as saying about one of them in this connection: "He writes about the human spirit as if it were a machine under the laws of mechanics; and, of course, what he says is perfectly intelligible, like any other treatise on matter; only what he says is not true! But I conceive of the soul in its living nature, as free, and intelligent, and sensitive; as under vital and not mechanical laws.' "

" . . . He simply refused to put infinite things into finite forms as wholly containing them. . . . Stated briefly, it was an exchange of definition for expression. His entrance into the company of New England theologians with such a theory was like Copernicus appearing among the Ptolemaists." (ps. 108-109). Light is thrown on this by what Harriet Beecher Stowe said in reference to the New England theology (whose chief exponent was Jonathan Edwards): "With all New England earnestness and practical efficiency, there is a long withering of the soul's more ethereal portion,—a crushing out of the beautiful,—which is horrible." [1]

Against the orthodoxy which they set up as final, Bushnell's independence of thought and heroic stand will be recalled: "I do peremptorily refuse to justify myself, as regards this matter of trinity, before any New England standard. We have no standard better than the residuary tri-theistic compost, such as may be left us after we have cast away that which alone made the old historic doctrine of trinity possible. I know not whether you design to make a standard for me of this decadent and dilapidated orthodoxy of ours; but if you do, then I appeal to Caesar; I

---

[1] Buckham, John Wright. *Progressive Religious Thought in America,* p. 9.

even undertake to arraign your standard itself before the tribunal of history." [1]

In this he was amply substantiated for, as one writer after another points out, he was much nearer the earlier theology than the New England hyper-orthodox group of his day. "Bushnell's discovery of his substantial agreement with the Nicene Creed was a satisfaction to him, not so much because it established his own orthodoxy, as that it revealed the heresy, not only of his critics, but of the entire New England School, if tested by the Nicene Creed." [2]

But he did more than reclothe ancient thought. "He was", as Dr. Munger says, "the first theologian in New England to admit fully into his thought the modern sense of nature, as it is found in the literature of the century, and notably in Wordsworth and Coleridge. . . . The secret of this movement was a spiritual interpretation of nature. It was a step in the evolution of human thought; and appearing first in literature, its natural point of entrance, it was sure to reach all forms of thought, as in time it will reach all forms of social life." [3]

"Those who know him only by his theological writings," said Bishop Clark, "have no conception of the range of his mind and the variety of subjects that he had investigated. He was skilled in mechanics, and has given the world some inventions of his own. The house in which I once lived was warmed by a furnace which he devised,

---

[1] Mead, Edwin D. *Horace Bushnell, the Citizen.* Boston, 1900. Reprint from the *New England Magazine*, Dec. 1899, and Jan. 1900. ps. 1-2.

[2] Munger, Theodore T. *Horace Bushnell: Preacher and Theologian.* op. cit. ps. 157-158.

[3] Ibid, ps. 381-382.

when such domestic improvements were comparatively new. He could plan a house or lay out a park or drain a city better than many of our experts. He was as much at home in talking with the rough guides of the Adirondacks as he was in discussing metaphysics with theologians in council. If he had been a medical man, he would have struck at the roots of disease and discovered remedies as yet unknown. If he had gone into civil life, he would have taught our public men some lessons in political economy which they greatly need to know.

"He led his class at Yale, we read, in athletic sports, as well as on the intellectual side; and he left in the college an enduring monument in the Beethoven Society, which he organized in order to lift the standard of the music in the chapel." [1]

In the section devoted to his California life, Dr. Munger says, "The variety of his studies and interests, especially in engineering and topography, reminds one of Da Vinci. If Bushnell had a passion outside of theology, it was for roads, and he closely connected the two; the new country afforded him a wide field for each. He was a critic of all he saw with the eye, and a builder in imagination of such as were needed or were possible. He foresaw a railroad across the continent,—hardly dreamed of as yet,—and, having examined all feasible routes of entrance into San Francisco, named the one that was finally chosen." [2]

At the Bushnell Centenary of the General Association of Connecticut in 1902, Charles Hopkins Clark, speaking on Bushnell the Citizen, called attention to his great interest

---

[1] Mead, Edwin D. *Horace Bushnell, the Citizen.* ps. 4 and 8.

[2] Munger, Theodore T. *Horace Bushnell: Preacher and Theologian* ps. 201-202.

in people. "Appealing in 1872 for a location of the state-house elsewhere than on the park itself, which had been decided upon, he actually, in a public meeting, reversed public opinion and started the movement that led to buying out Trinity College and placing the building on the old college grounds. In his speech he said:

" 'My friends, I have done something for this city because I love Hartford, and have tried to give some evidence of it in what I did to secure this park. And how I have got my pay I will tell you. I have been on the park and seen there the humble people,—now an old man, feeble and tottering, going to rest himself, and then have looked upon a sickly woman and her child, who had no bright spot at home, who had come out here to breathe and see one of God's smiles, and they did see it. I have got my pay in that way. They none of them knew me; therefore the more I enjoyed their joy. They didn't know that I had anything to do with getting the park, and it was best that they did not as I walked along.' " [1]

Williston Walker declared that "At the present day no view advocated by Dr. Bushnell has won so wide acceptance among the churches or theological schools of our order as that set forth in his 'Christian Nurture'." He added this: "Dr. Bushnell's particular interpretation of the Trinity, and his modifications of view regarding it, are, however, relatively unimportant. The great fact is that he sought to take the doctrine out of the realm of intellectual speculation into that of Christian experience and to find its essence in the truth 'that God is a being practi-

---

[1] Bushnell Centenary. *Minutes of the General Association of Connecticut,* at the one hundred and ninety-third annual meeting, held in Hartford, June 17-18, 1902. ps. 67-68.

cally related to his creatures.' " [1]   This was a revolutionary change.

Dr. Joseph H. Twichell, who had been brought up in Hartford and was therefore intimate with his whole life, returned to become the minister in a neighboring church during the last years of Bushnell's life.   At the Centenary Dr. Twichell gave some personal reminiscences, in one of which he shows the source of Bushnell's inspiration and power.   "Few of my recollections of him are so dear, and none are more precious, than of his prayers; pre-eminently of some I heard him offer in the sanctuary of nature.   One of these in particular is deep-graven in my memory. . . . The Doctor was thoroughly fatigued with his climb, and so I found him a seat beside the basin pool below the falls, and rigged out a rod for him and left him to catch trout for supper,—which he did in sufficiency, though he said he was too tired to see the water—while I prepared our bed and made a fire.   When it came time to get into our blankets we had a few verses from the New Testament . . . and then I asked him to pray.   He turned partly over on his face—he was lying down—and began in his natural voice but with a tone as soft and melodious as the low murmur of the stream beneath, what seemed for all the world like speaking to some one who was next to him, but whom I did not see.   And so he continued communing in expressions of adoring thanks and love and humility and trust and blessed hope with that near Presence, till, when he ceased, I found every other thought swallowed up in the feeling that God was there.   There was in it all the vivid suggestion, the reflection, of a long and dear acquaint-

---

[1] Bushnell Centenary.   Address, "Dr. Bushnell as a Religious Leader". ps. 24 and 30.

ance fraught with holy memories—as, indeed, there was—between him and his God—his God in Christ." [1]

Again and again writers and speakers come back to *Christian Nurture* as peculiarly significant and abiding. "Of all of Dr. Bushnell's writings," said Charles E. McKinley at the Centennial, "those on Christian Nurture were most convincing, and therefore most influential. The series began with an article on 'Revivals of Religion', published in 1836. [2] The two discourses on 'What Christian Nurture Is' appeared ten years later." (p. 100).

Bushnell's writings are full of aphorisms. This is characteristic of all literary geniuses. Dr. Munger published a number of them in the special Bushnell anniversary number of *The Congregationalist and Christian World* of June 7, 1902 [3]; and Mrs. Mary Bushnell Cheney has included some forty pages of them in the volume of his sermons entitled *The Spirit in Man*, ps. 403-444. [4] His "Picture of a Wise Man" [5] is quite famous. Of this Dr. Munger says, in the magazine referred to above: "If everything of Bushnell shall be forgotten or blotted out—sermon, treatise and essay—let this page remain as the sign of a great master in the use of language, and also as such a measure of manhood and sound thinking as he set up and strove to realize." (p. 813, footnote).

In this number of the magazine, Dr. Reuen Thomas of England gives a charming picture of a week in Hartford

---

[1] Bushnell Centenary. Address, "Personal Reminiscences". ps. 81-82.

[2] The date of this article is 1838.

[3] Vol. LXXXVII, No. 23. The Pilgrim Press. Boston and Chicago. A Bushnell number. ps. 812-813.

[4] Centenary edition. New York, Charles Scribner's Sons. 1903.

[5] In magazine just quoted, p. 813; and in *Spirit in Man*, p. 444.

and his many walks and talks with Bushnell. "He had received a check for $2,000 from some English publisher. . . . When I told him of the extent of his influence in England and that all young ministers of any alertness of mind, in all denominations, read his books . . . he was so surprised that for a while I think he was suspicious of my veracity. . . . I walked with Bushnell through the park. His conversation was as stimulating as his books. . . . His delight in having been the chief instrument of converting 'a place for garbage and dead dogs and cats' into a beautiful park was too evident to be suppressed. 'They will put your name on this park, doctor,' I remarked. 'O no, O no, people in this country soon forget their benefactors'. But he lived long enough—just long enough—to know that my prediction was verified. . . . It has been said by cynical souls that if you wish to keep your interest in an author's book it is better you should not be personally familiar with your author. After that week with Bushnell his books were more precious to me than ever." [1]

One other characteristic of liberal thinking is that one must ever keep the open mind and be ready, as in science, to reconstruct one's findings. Dr. Thomas throws light on Bushnell's attitude in this respect. "One conversation in particular I recall. It was about his books on the atonement. I asked if the two volumes, entitled 'Vicarious Sacrifice' and 'Forgiveness and Law', satisfied him that the whole theme had now been reviewed by him. He replied: 'By no means. If I got fresh light tomorrow I would recall these books whatever the publisher might say.' " (p. 814).

In this same magazine are brief statements of "Personal Indebtedness to Horace Bushnell; a group of testi-

---

[1] Ibid, p. 814. "My Week with Dr. Bushnell".

monies from men who have been quickened and inspired by him." (ps. 815-816). From these a few sentences are culled:

"His temper, his eagerness for truth, his open-mindedness and pure-heartedness, his love for all that is human, except sin, and his enthronement of the Master, all profoundly affected me, and do still. . . . The man is always a force, and to him I return again and again." [1]

"Dr. Bushnell's persistent note of scrupulous honesty and reality in Christian thinking and living I particularly prize. One has no chance ever to feel that he is simply going through the motions. It would be difficult to overestimate his contribution—direct and indirect—to American religious thinking." [2]

"He was a rare man. I do not know any one with whom to compare him. He was a fearless seer, a diligent observer, an honest prophet, who dared do anything with truth save to doubt or disobey." [3]

The great swing towards Bushnell's ideas in theology is brought out by Lewis O. Brastow in his *Representative Modern Preachers*, in which he says: "Dr. Bushnell was a theologian and has left behind a theology sufficiently distinctive to bear his name. It is a curious turn in the course of events that our theological institutions, as in a sort of defence of the Christian faith, should to-day be expounding the theology of a man who spent his life in antagonizing theology, and who denied that anything like a system of theology is possible." [4]

---

[1] William F. McDowell, New York, N. Y., p. 815.

[2] Henry Churchill King, Oberlin, Ohio, p. 815.

[3] Alexander McKenzie, Cambridge, Mass., p. 815.

[4] The Macmillan Co., New York, 1904, p. 146.

As a preacher he is classed with Beecher and Brooks and in many respects placed above them. He is considered their superior in literary form by many and also in solidity and strength. "His preaching had a more solid quality, and aggregated a larger amount of important truth, than that of Beecher or Brooks. All of these preachers were ingenious in homiletic suggestion. They spoke to the imagination and stirred an emotional interest in the truths discussed. But Bushnell has the greater strength." (p. 163).

Phillips Brooks had something of the large-heartedness and outlook on life that Bushnell delighted in. That he owed some of his inspiration to Bushnell is undoubted. "Taking the sonnets of Brooks as indications of his grateful recognition to those who contributed to his growth, mention should be made of Dr. Bushnell, to whom a sonnet is also addressed. No books in Brooks's library show signs of harder usage than Bushnell's *Sermons for the New Life,* and Maurice's *Theological Essays.*" [1]

Williston Walker gives Bushnell place on his roll of "Great Men in the Christian Church." [2] He says: "Bushnell was not a theologian in the sense in which that designation may be applied to Edwards. He had no desire to be. He wrought out no close-argued logical system. He believed none possible, and he regarded it as the chief evil of contemporary theology that men had made the endeavor. He founded no school. No party calls itself by his name. But he had a poet's fire of imagination, and a prophet's perception of the reality of God. He strove to reach back be-

[1] Allen, Alexander V. G. *Phillips Brooks. 1835-1893.* Memories of his life with extracts from his letters and note-books. New York, E. P. Dutton and Co., 1907. p. 66.

[2] Constructive Bible Studies, Advanced and supplementary series. Chicago, The University of Chicago Press, 1908. Chapter XX "Horace Bushnell", ps. 368-369.

yond the formulas in which his contemporaries believed
Christian truth to be absolutely defined to the greater spiritual verities which they and he alike felt, but which he
regarded their formulas as merely symbolizing and often-
times misrepresenting. He sought to make the presentation
of Christianity simpler and more natural. In so doing, he
made easy for many the transition from the older to the
newer conceptions of the Christian faith." And he con-
siders Bushnell has "an abiding position in the history of
American religious thought."

Bushnell was one of these people whom William James
later referred to as above price because rich in germinal
ideas. Today they would be called creative. This very
quality—"a new ferment"—is brought out by Dr. Charles
F. Dole in an article in *The New World*. "Aside from the
vigor and charm of his style, these books . . . were a new
ferment in religious thought through the middle of the
century. No more subtly disintegrating force ever touched
the old Calvinistic theology of New England in its strong-
holds. [1] . . . The faith for which he really stood and toward
which he made as gallant a struggle as the nature of his
mind permitted, was as different from that which had held
New England for two centuries in bondage as if it had
borne the name of a new religion. It was and is indeed a
new religion. It is the religion of character and reason;
it is the religion of humanity; it is the religion of the living
God. . . . I prefer to say frankly that it is the religion of
the ideal Christ; that is, the divine person that waits to be
in the soul of every man,—our highest possible image of the

---

[1] "Horace Bushnell and His Work for Theology". Reprint from
The New World. Houghton, Mifflin Co. The Riverside Press, Cambridge. Vol. 8, 1899. p. 699.

likeness of God, incarnate in manhood. This must be, under whatever name it shall assume, the religion of the future. Toward this larger religion, which shall include all true-hearted men and women, Bushnell in an age of confused thought was a very worthy though not a far-sighted contributor." (p. 714).

Few "classics" are produced in any century. To write one confers an immortality greatly longed for by authors. Bushnell was probably innocent of any such ambition, and yet not a few would agree with Grenville Kleiser that *Christian Nurture* is "a book now looked upon as of classical authority." He says that Bushnell's "influence upon the ministers of America in modifying theology and remolding the general type of preaching is fairly comparable with that of Robertson." [1]

George Albert Coe is the greatest leader in this field to-day. He wrote: [2]

"A child can, to use Bushnell's words, grow up a Christian, and never know himself as being otherwise. . . . To Tertullian's argument that the soul is naturally Christian we may now add that the child is naturally Christian. To the Christian idea of the All-Father the response (unless the child has already been wounded and scarred by the un-parental conduct of others) is positive, free, and vital. Children love and trust him; they struggle to obey him by kindly conduct; they desire to help him in his work; they are grateful for his gifts."

"It is possible," says another, "that a mediating thinker like Horace Bushnell had as much influence, perhaps more,

[1] *The World's Great Sermons.* Vol. 4. L. Beecher to Bushnell. Funk and Wagnalls, New York and London, 1908. p. 234.

[2] A Social Theory of Religious Education. Charles Scribner's Sons, New York, 1919. Page 145.

in making Christianity the permeating force of modern life than the sermon-polemics of Lyman Beecher." He held that "the spirit of man was the candle of the Lord and could make a path of bright reality through the eternal mystery. He was guided by his heart and not by the logic that filled the air about him. Many will agree with a writer in the New York *Tribune* that 'Every Man's Life a Plan of God' is one of the greatest sermons of the English-speaking pulpit." [1]

He points out another characteristic which fore-shadows part of "the social Gospel" of later years. "Horace Bushnell did not fear to preach politics in the pulpit. Men were measuring duty by apparent consequence and so fearing to say a word for the slave. But Bushnell maintained that righteousness secured the only consequences worth having." (p. 254).

Chief among the "liberators and pioneers" in America, according to John Wright Buckham, is Horace Bushnell. He adds, "We go back constantly to such minds not only to secure more comprehensive insights but for fresh impetus and incentive. . . . The last twenty-five years have witnessed a greatly enhanced estimate of his part in theological advance and a fresh sense of the unexhausted treasures of his productive personality." [2]

The first point in emancipation according to Buckham was his conviction "that the life of God is in the life of the race." (p. 10).

---

[1] Hoyt, Arthur S. *The Pulpit and American Life.* New York, The Macmillan Co., 1921. ps. 180-181.

[2] *Progressive Religious Thought in America.* A survey of the enlarging Pilgrim faith. Houghton, Mifflin Co., The Riverside Press, Cambridge, 1919. ps. 6-7.

The second is to substitute experience for cold rationalism, so securing release from the galling chains of theological definitions. He relies in part on intuition and finds a mystical quality in the New Testament and in the world.

The third "great deliverance ... lay in breaking down the dividing wall between nature and the supernatural." (p. 20). Both are one system, but he maintains "the priority and worth of personality as a supernatural reality." (p. 22).

Finally, he did much to recover the personality of Jesus. [1]

There are, of course, "external and visible marks" of Bushnell in Hartford. Dr. Edwin P. Parker in *The Congregationalist and Christian World* of June 7, 1902, the centenary of Bushnell's birth, gives five of these, namely, "the old North Church Meeting House; ... the house which he built and in which he lived and died (on Winthrop Street) ; . . . The Park Church Meeting House; . . . The state capitol . . . in the location of which he was deeply concerned, and which bears his effigy cut in one of the medallions in its eastern wall; . . . and the beautiful park in the heart of the city, which is his enduring civic monument." [2] He omitted mentioning the grave in the Old North Church Cemetery. Of these visible marks the first three are gone, though the tablet erected in his honor in Park Church is preserved in the new Horace Bushnell Memorial Hall. This magnificent Hall, seating over three thousand people, was opened in 1930 and dedicated to the citizens of

---

[1] P. 25. See especially his "God in Christ", "Nature and the Supernatural", "The Vicarious Sacrifice".

[2] Vol. LXXXVII, No. 23. Pilgrim Press, Boston and Chicago, A Bushnell number. "Dr. Bushnell's Marks in Hartford". p. 817.

Hartford. It has, in the opinion of many people, changed the city from something of a provincial town to a cosmopolitan centre, with operas, oratorios and symphony concerts; and lecturers and preachers speaking on great scientific, social and religious themes. Bushnell Hall became at once not merely a hall, but an institution, appealing to the imagination and rooted in the lives of the people. It is an enduring memorial promoting many of the interests and ideals for which Bushnell stood.

Unfortunately there is little reference to *Christian Nurture* in his latest biography but what is said of his theological views and especially of the Atonement applies equally well to the earlier work. Indeed, most of what was developed later in books and sermons more strictly theological is implicit in *Christian Nurture*. "Bushnell's theory of the Atonement is of great importance and vast formative influence among the historic doctrines of the Atonement. It is not too much to say that probably most of the men in the progressive groups today build their idea of the Atonement on Bushnell's thought and conception." [1]

The Atlantic Monthly, March, 1900, in reviewing Dr. Munger's biography, says of Bushnell: "This man would have been a discoverer of new truth and liberator in whatever station he was set. By instinct he was a pioneer, adventurous, fearless, requiring no leader, content to stand alone and to advance alone if deserted by followers."

Concerning *Christian Nurture* the writer says: "As a substitute for—or better, a correction of—the too great dependence of the churches, for their replenishment, upon so-called 'revivals of religion', Bushnell asserted the pos-

---

[1] Archibald, Warren Seymour. *Horace Bushnell*. Hartford, E. V. Mitchell, 1930. p. 91.

sibility and duty of so educating the souls of children that they will develop characters in harmony with the divine character, cheerfully obedient to the Christian law of life, and gravitating to acceptance of the responsibility of church membership in due season, without awful paroxysms of conscience or cataclysmal drenchings by the Holy Spirit. He denied that the change of heart, theologically termed conversion, must be 'the product of separate and absolutely independent choice.' " [1]

Rev. E. M. Chapman in a review of Munger's biography entitled "God's Way With a Soul" in *The Congregationalist* of September 21, 1899, writes: "All things considered, the volume on Christian Nurture is probably the most important that Bushnell ever wrote. I have said that its thesis ought to prove almost as startling today as it was in 1847; not because it threatens the integrity of our theological system—we have scarcely enough theological system to be threatened—but because its practical implications are so terribly neglected. The most casual reader of *Horace Bushnell, Preacher and Theologian* will perceive its author's earnest purpose to direct the attention of pastors, teachers and, above all, parents to this little volume, with its "infinite riches in a narrow room'; and he who reads it will be inclined to agree with Dr. Munger's feeling as expressed not long since in a letter to a friend: 'That book is the most needed book today. It is more needed today than when first written.' " [2]

Dr. Munger, personal friend and biographer of Bushnell, was also perhaps the most profound student of his

---

[1] Vol. LXXXV. No. DIX. "Horace Bushnell" by Walter Allen. ps. 415-417.
[2] Vol. LXXXIV, No. 38. Boston. p. 397.

work. Writing over fifty years after the publication of the
little volume which caused such a stir, and long after the
passions of controversy had died out, he gave this reasoned
judgment: "Few people in New England would now hesi-
tate to say that it is wise to train children into the Christian
life very much as Bushnell suggests; and the greater part
would wonder where the theological difficulties came in." [1]

"It is enough to say that 'Christian Nurture' has slowly
and quietly supplanted revivalism in New England,—not
the thing itself, for it still lingers in a harmless and often
useful and even necessary way, but it has taught the
churches that the law of their growth does not lie in revivals, but in the Christian nurture of the young. The
theological objections to it vanished long ago, and it has
passed into the religious life of New England as a permeating and transforming influence. The revival system
would have worn itself out in time through contact with
modern ideas and methods, but it would have left the
churches without a doctrine of Christian growth, and also
without a working method. 'Christian Nurture' furnished
both, and saved the church from that worst of all fates, the
loss of a vital doctrine without one to fill its place. But
even a greater achievement of this book was that it so
effectively turned the current of Christian thought toward
the young, where it is now going and must continue to go."
(ps. 389-390).

And now a generation later, these words are even
more nearly a statement of fact than when they were
spoken. The verdict of history is singularly clear and
decisive.

---

[1] *Horace Bushnell: Preacher and Theologian.* p. 92.

In his book *A History of Religious Education in Connecticut to the Middle of the Nineteenth Century* Dr. George Stewart, after a careful study of the whole sweep of the years wrote: "The idea of Christian nurture, as set forth by Horace Bushnell, in contrast to the revivalistic theory of the churches, was the outstanding contribution to religious education in the middle of the last century. To Bushnell, more than to any other educational or religious leader in Connecticut, belongs the credit for dignifying the instruction of children in religious matters and for emphasizing the importance of training in early years for growth into Christian character. . . . This conception of religious education had a profound effect not only in Connecticut but in religious circles throughout the country. . . . Bushnell's conception of the religious education of the young opened an opportunity to give children consistent and permanent instruction adapted to their ages. Before his time there had existed only the spasmodic and fugitive attempts of a church which looked upon revivals as the chief means of recruiting for Protestant Christianity." [1]

Luther A. Weigle, who as Horace Bushnell professor at Yale Divinity School, is able to speak with some authority on his life and work sums up in these words: "The modern movement for the better religious education of children owes more to Horace Bushnell, doubtless, than to any other one man. His 'Christian Nurture' was in sober truth an epoch-making book. In it he sharply criticized the extreme individualism, the reliance upon emotional revivals, and the one-sided supernaturalism which had characterized the thought and practice of American churches

[1] New Haven, Yale University Press, 1924. ps. 347 and 366.

throughout the second half of the eighteenth and the first half of the nineteenth centuries; and he vindicated for childhood its normal place in the Kingdom of God, and for the family its function as the instrument, by God's grace, of Christian nurture.

" . . . It is remarkable in how many respects Bushnell's dissent from current theories and practices anticipated the development of later days. He opposed what was called 'indoctrination', which consisted chiefly in the memorization of dogmatic catechisms, and favored a larger emphasis upon the understanding of Scripture; he advocated the graduation of methods and materials of instruction in Christian truth; he recommended greater freedom in conversation with respect to the objects of religious belief, and more sincerity in answering children's questions and in dealing with adolescent doubts; he believed that the play of children, instead of being a symptom of original sin, is a 'divine appointment', of educative value, and 'the symbol and interpreter of Christian liberty'; he conceived the goal of education in terms of what he called 'the emancipation of the child.' " [1]

Bushnell was not showered with honors. He wrote " 'My figure in this world has not been great, but I have had a great experience. I have never been a great agitator, never pulled a wire to get the will of men, never did a politic thing. It was not for this reason, but because I was looked upon as a singularity—not exactly sane, perhaps in many things—that I was almost never a president or vice-president of any society and almost never on a committee.

---

[1] *Religious Education.* Vol. XIX. February, 1924—December, 1924. "The Christian Ideal of Family Life as Expounded in Horace Bushnell's 'Christian Nurture'." ps. 47 and 55.

Take the report of my doings on the platform of the world's business and it is naught! I have filled no place at all. But still it has been a great thing for me to live.' "

And, continues his latest biographer, [1] "this power of the imagination gives us the clue to his greatness. For Horace Bushnell was a great character. . . . He belongs to his age, and he belongs to all the ages. . . .

"Let us, then, praise famous men, for of such is the true commonwealth, where no race, no time, no land divides, and where the truth unites."

There is no doubt that the appeal to history more than justifies Bushnell and assures him a safe place. He was truly a prophet or as he preferred expressing it, "one of God's experimenters."

---

[1] Archibald, Warren Seymour. Horace Bushnell, Hartford, Connecticut. E. V. Mitchell, 1930. ps. 147 and 154-5.

APPENDIX

1. Table of Contents to Rev. J. Janeway's book *A Token for Children.*

EXAMPLE I.—Of one eminently converted, between eight and nine years old, with an account of her life and death

EXAMPLE II.—Of a child admirably affected with the things of God, when between two and three years old, with a brief account of his life and death

EXAMPLE III.—Of a little girl that was wrought upon when between four and five years old, with some account of her holy life, and triumphant death

EXAMPLE IV.—Of a child that began to look towards heaven when she was about four years old; with some observable passages in her life, and at her death

EXAMPLE V.—Of the pious life and joyful death of a child, when he was about twelve years old

EXAMPLE VI.—Of a poor child that was awakened when he was five years old

EXAMPLE VII.—Of a notorious wicked child, that was taken up from begging, and admirably converted; with an account of his holy life, and joyful death, when he was about nine years old

EXAMPLE VIII.—Of a child that was very serious at four years old; with an account of his comfortable death, when he was twelve years and three weeks old

EXAMPLE IX.—Of a child that was very eminent when she was between five and six years old, with some memorable passages of her life

EXAMPLE X.—Of a child that was awakened when she was between seven and eight years old; with some account of her last hours, and triumphant death

EXAMPLE XI.—Of a child greatly affected with the things of God, when very young; with an account of her admirable carriage upon her death-bed.

EXAMPLE XII.—Of the excellent carriage of a child upon his death-bed, when about seven years old

EXAMPLE XIII.—Of one that began to look towards heaven, when he was very young; with many eminent passages of his life, and joyful death, when he was eleven and three-quarters old.

2. Bushnell's letter to his daughter, from Geneva, dated October 6, 1845.

"My dear Child,— . . . How much I long to see you I cannot tell. No earthly prospect is so bright to me as to be once more in our pleasant, happy home, where I may hear the voices of my dear children, and see them gathered at our simple table, saying Father and Mother as before I left them. I think of you at night; every child and family call you to mind by day. . . . You are now precisely of the age to study, and there is nothing I so much desire for you on earth as that you may have a truly accomplished mind and character.

"But if intelligence is necessary to make a fine woman, other things are quite as necessary. Her mind and heart must be perfectly pure, as that of infancy. She must be the very expression of modesty, and without the least affectation in her manners.

"Therefore I am anxious, my dear daughter, that you should begin the Christian life now and grow up in it. If I have proposed to you something angelic in the model of a woman, I am far enough from believing that any mere self-cultivation will enable you to reach it. Such is man and woman, such all human nature, that only grace can raise it into beauty and true goodness. Man is not so good or susceptible to good that he can fill out the ideal of goodness without proximity to God, or drawing himself up to his mark by the assimilating power of God's love and communion. . . . Be it, then, your first thought to be religious; your girlhood, and thus your womanhood,—your whole life, and thus your death and all beyond." [1]

The next is from Hartford, January 17, 1848:

"My dear Child,—You can hardly guess how much we miss you. When our little circle is gathered round the parlor fire at evening, we all take turns saying,—perhaps breaking silence to say,—I wish now dear L—— was here. And the children ask, moreover, how long, how many months, will it be before she comes home? And then I see how their souls are stretching and working after the measures of time, contriving in themselves how long a month is, and how long these months will be. Well, it is a blessed thing for them to know the measures of time through their affections,—how much better than to learn its measures through expectations of pleasure, appetite, or any selfish good. If we all had our clock in our hearts, measuring off our days by the love we exercise to friends, to mankind, and to God,

---

[1] Cheney, Mrs. Mary Bushnell. *Life and Letters of Horace Bushnell*, New York, Harper and Bros., 1880. ps. 139-143.

we should make a friend of time also. We should live, in
fact, a great while longer in a much shorter time.

". . . You have been religiously educated, and you are
come now to an age when you must begin to be more responsible to yourself. Our prayer for you is, every day,
that God would impart his grace to you and draw you on
to a full choice of himself, and perform the good work
which we trust he has begun in you. This would complete
our happiness in you. I would recommend to you now that
you set before you, as a distinct object, the preparing yourself to make a profession of the Saviour. Make this a distinct object of thought and of prayer every day. And do
not inquire so much what you are, whether truly a Christian in heart or not, as how you may come into the full
Christian spirit, to become unselfish, to have a distinct
and abiding love to Christ. Unite yourself to Christ for
life, and try to receive his beautiful and loving spirit. . . .
Pray God, also, to give you his spirit, and do not doubt
that his spirit will help you through all difficulties. In all
your duties and studies, endeavor to do them for God and
so as to please him. Make this, too, your pleasure, for
assuredly it will be the highest pleasure. It may not so
appear at first, but it will be so very soon. Nothing, you
will see in a moment, can yield so sweet a pleasure as the
love and pursuit of excellence, especially that excellence
which consists in a good and right heart before God. And
you will be more likely to love this work and have success
in it, if you set before you some fixed object, such as I
have proposed.

"We gave you to God in your childhood, and now it
belongs to you to thank God for the good we have sought

to do for you, and try to fulfil our kindness by assuming for yourself what we promised for you. . . . May the good spirit of God, my dear child, guide you in your absence from us, be with you daily, and assist you to be wise. May every day be a happy day, because it is passed under the smile of your heavenly Father.

"Your loving father,

Horace Bushnell." (ps. 188-190).

THE END